Joy in the Journey

Joy in the Journey

81 Devotions

by Arnold G. Kuntz

CONCORDIA
PUBLISHING HOUSE

Cover photo 1–Paul Barton, 2–Edgeworth Prods.,
3–Jon Feingersh; The Stock Market.

Copyright © 1992 Concordia Publishing House
3558 S. Jefferson Avenue, St. Louis, MO 63118-3968
Manufactured in the United States of America

Library of Congress Cataloging-in-Publication Data

Kuntz, Arnold G., 1926–
    Joy in the journey: devotions / by Arnold G. Kuntz.
    ISBN 0-570-04576-2
    1. Aged—Prayer-books and devotions—English. I. Title.
    BV4580.K86   1992
    242' .65—dc20   92-3675
                                    CIP

1 2 3 4 5 6 7 8 9 10 VP 01 00 99 98 97 96 95 94 93 92

Contents

Preface

One of the discoveries of growing up and old is that life keeps getting filled with more and more meaning as our understanding matures. It's very special to have arrived at senior status. Given enough time, of course, everybody can get there. But you and I have arrived. It calls for a unique and special devotional relationship with that great and gracious God who has let us live so long and experience so much.

The offerings in this little volume are intended for personal use and seek to open up the consciousness to a lot of unworded and often unuttered yearnings lurking in our secret hearts. I earnestly hope that you find much of your own experience here, and yourself in devotional conversations with God.

Arnold G. Kuntz

Red Alert

As they were walking along the road, a man said to [Jesus], "I will follow wherever you go." Luke 9:57

Actually there were three men in the story (Luke 9:57–62), but this one makes the point. You take a risk when you join the company of Christ. Jesus is literally surrounded by companions. You and I are among them. There is no counting the number who have walked with Christ across the centuries. Just to be with him, just to listen to him speak, is to be reckoned among the great privileges of life. But beware; at least be aware: it takes a rare combination of callous indifference and what might mistakenly be termed "good luck" to come away from listening to Jesus unscathed, though I am amazed how many people seem to manage it. The man in our text was having a perfectly delightful and inspiring time listening to Jesus as they strolled along when suddenly his whole life was brought up short. Who knows why he had come to be with Christ. Maybe he had a vague interest in a somewhat famous man. Maybe he wanted to give the impression of being "Sunday morning" pious. It's not important. What is important is that something happened once he was there. After listening to Jesus for a while, he ended up saying, "I will follow wherever you go."

Never say I didn't warn you. Walking with Jesus you run the risk that something will happen, something stupendous. Jesus may very well spark in you the irresistible urge to follow him. You can end up saying, "I will follow wherever you go." It's happened before and it will happen again. Hang around Jesus and you could suddenly end up committed to following him wherever he may lead.

Prayer

Eternal Father, whose I am and whom I serve because Christ Jesus leads me, move my heart to follow him, my feet to walk his paths and my life to serve you in everlasting righteousness. Amen.

Try This

Put it on the line, that one thing you will do today because you are following Jesus wherever he goes.

In Sickness and in Health

The Lord is close to the brokenhearted and saves those who are crushed in spirit. Psalm 34:18

Christians like to talk about how useful their faith is for mending broken hearts and healing wounded feelings. Our faith pulls us through sickness and keeps us steady in the midst of stress. We like to think of our faith in terms of health and strength.

But, having said that, it's interesting to note that the opposite is at least as true. Phrases which express and describe physical infirmity can be appropriate descriptions, too, of what Christianity is all about. Some words, some idioms used to denote illness in Christian terminology stand for spiritual health. Here is one: A broken heart. Our hearts go out to the brokenhearted. We do all we can to help the one whose heart is broken. If it were left to us we'd just as soon not have one, thank you. Yet, in Christian parlance the broken heart is a symbol of something good, desirable, something every Christian must possess. It is, after all, the broken heart which God will not despise. God will not scale that great pile of self-righteousness which blocks the entrance to our hearts.

God makes himself known to the humble and comes with comfort and forgiveness and renewal to those who understand how badly they have slipped and how far they have fallen, and then, not giving up, look around for help, find it in God, go to him for forgiveness and ask for his hand to lift them out of their despair. "I, a poor miserable sinner, confess to you all my sins." That's the attitude of Christianity, a broken and a contrite heart. God enters our hearts through the cracks and breaks in them which make us need him.

Prayer

Savior of the human race, you find us in our extremities and bring us rescue. You have come to save the weak and helpless. Let no pride in any wholeness or wellness of my own keep me from the gifts of forgiveness and renewal which you bring to those who seek you. Come to me and heal me. Amen.

Try This

Some physical maladies are symbols of Christian strength. Here are a few: Color-blindness, near-sightedness, far-sightedness, thin skin. In what way do these words and phrases describe Christian health?

A New Dawn

I will awaken the dawn. Psalm 57:8

"She'll Be Comin' Round the Mountain" is not found in any anthology of Christian hymns. Maybe it should be. It has a distinctive Christian flavor. Christian hymns are often a forecast of things to come. In the hymnal with which I am most familiar there are six hymns cataloged specifically as hymns of watchfulness and five more listed under the title "Coming of the Lord." Christianity has been called many things, but this is probably the first time it has been compared to a train whistle, a tuneful horn in the night, a proclamation that something is coming round the mountain, something is topping the crest of the hill, something wonderful is pending from the side of heaven.

"I will awaken the dawn." Please note, not "I will wait for it." I'll bring it about, hurry it up, awaken it. Mankind has in its possession plenty which makes for darkness. Wars, and rumors of them; technology which forever drags in with it, it seems, the things which depress the spirit and produce the tragedies whose headlines dominate the front page of our papers. There is a whole new area of research headed up by a professor in San Diego which is seeking to find ways to ensure that people are served by technology and not the other way around.

There are exotic, new diseases which have swept ahead of our ability to control them. They are the product of man's doing too, some of them. Oh, we can make it dark. And we can bring about false dawns: the post-war world, the promise of nuclear power, a growth economy; lots of promise and plenty of disappointment.

But we can also bring the dawn. We can by word and deed hasten a new day. We can bring light to people who are still engulfed in the gloom of night. We can carry Christ's lamp into the dark and awaken those who need a new dawn in which the sun of righteousness rises with healing in his wings.

Prayer

Empower me, Light of our world, to do those things and say those words which hasten the dawn and illuminate the hearts of people with the promise of your grace.

Try This

Select one person for each day of the week into whose life you will bring a ray of light.

Both Root and Destiny

Jesus knew that . . . he had come from God and was returning to God. John 13:3

It seems to me it would be decidedly to our advantage to spend a little more time exploring all those things which indicate our kinship with God and a whole lot less groveling around trying to prove that we are linked to some scaly fish which one day flopped up out of the sea. We don't need biologists to explain why we behave the way we do nearly as much as we need seers to tell us why, now and again, we behave like decent people and then some. "A little lower than the angels" (Heb. 2:7). There is something in us which is tuned to the wave length of our God.

13

"Jesus knew that . . . he had come from God and was returning to God." That's why he grabbed a towel and began to wash feet (John 13:5). You travel on the same track. God is the one who set you up in business on this earth and, when it's all been said and done, God is the one who will take you back. Jesus' origins, of course, are a whole lot loftier than ours. He is God's son, and not just in a manner of speaking. It can be said of us too, however, that "it is he who hath made us, and not we ourselves" (Ps. 100:3, KJV). We aren't any vague accident coupled with enough time so that all the pieces fall into place to spell our names. Given such roots, our destiny is comfortingly lofty too. Not just a "tale told by an idiot . . . signifying nothing." We're on our way to the Father. That makes a difference. That gives life a purpose and invests it with a style.

The next time you are inclined to ask what your life is all about, try this on for size: God set me here, not for what I can get out of it but what I can give. I'm here not to make a living but a life, a life in him, and when it's done, I'm going back to him, and none too soon, if I have my way—and his.

Prayer

To you, my Father strong to save, ruler of life and death, be praise now and forever. Amen.

Try This

Identify three events in your life, things you have done, which indicate your roots and destiny are with God, any "deed of kindness done."

First Faith . . .

Make every effort to add to your faith . . . . 2 Peter
1:5

It all starts with faith. You don't start in the middle and work back. It isn't a matter of being decent or kind or truthful and from there you find your way back to God in Jesus. No. It starts with faith. It begins like the burst of a new day with firm reliance on the revelation that God, in his Son, Jesus, has done for you what you cannot do for yourself. That he has made good for all your blots and blunders and the downright inexcusable sins which shame you bitterly when you look back at them. That he has made all things new for you. On top of that you put the results of that faith which inevitably ensue.

If you look up that 2 Peter passage in your Bible, you'll find the first thing that follows faith is virtue. You have to look for them, but here and there in this world of ours, you come upon virtuous men and women. These are the folks who watch their language, are reasonably honest, and help the elderly at street corners. But Christian virtue never exists in a vacuum. It begins with the mind-boggling, earth-shattering, life-changing discovery that God "will remember [our] sins no more" (Jer. 31:34) because he handled that matter already on Calvary. To that discovery you add virtue, which is nothing less than a change in attitude from self-concern to love. "By this all men will know that you are [a person of faith], if you love one another" (John 13:35). And that goes a great deal farther than not cheating on your income tax. That love reaches out to the homeless and destitute, the brokenhearted and diseased, and the hateful and forsaken, too, with compassion and patience and understanding. That love takes self, your self, out of the middle of things. But the point is, it starts with faith, with belief in and commitment to the Son of God. To that you add virtue.

Prayer

Great active agent of my salvation and my life, add to my faith virtue. My faith waits on you for any good in me. Amen.

Try This

Honesty, kindness, generosity are virtues. Isolate from your week some deed of kindness done. Why did you do it? Was it specifically because of your love for Jesus? Was it an addition to faith?

When God Says Nothing

Jesus did not answer a word. Matthew 15:23, KJV

Ordinarily it is the words of God which impress us. We spend a lot of time studying his word. He caused thousands of words to be written "for our learning." Now and again, however, he doesn't say anything. That can be a problem. It can push a person to the very edge of his faith. More than one is troubled by the silence of our God. St. Paul mutters, "Three times I pleaded, but . . . " All he got was a cryptic, "My grace is sufficient for you" (2 Cor. 12:9). Still, that was an improvement over what the mother got in our text. "Jesus did not answer a word."

The silence of God can at times be as eloquent as any of his words. Please don't ever think that God's silence is a sign that he has ceased to care. This is, after all, God we are talking about, the one who left his throne on high and turned it in for a bale of hay, because he cares. This is the one who stood mute as soldiers slapped and guards spit and the priests of the people jeered, because he cares. "He hath borne our griefs, and carried our sorrows" (Is. 53:4, KJV). Oh, he cares. So that isn't it, when he doesn't say a word to you.

Abraham concluded that it was a test. He took his son and tied him up and raised the knife (Gen. 22:1–13), certain that what God would do or wouldn't is always good. Any botanist, and Abraham, too, will tell you that trees strike deep roots when they stand against strong winds. Sometimes God's silence is a test, a test of faith. Simon Peter learned, as he stood in the shadows off to the corner of the courtyard, that silence can convict (Luke 22:61). It became so deathly silent in that courtyard you could hear the cock crow outside the city walls. God's silence can convict. But above all God's silence gently calls. His silence is wonderful to listen to. "Be still, and know that I am God" (Ps. 46:10). Set aside the distractions and the perplexities which clamor in your ears. God loves you. Listen in the quiet to him. God is always calling to you, even when you think that God says nothing.

Prayer
Lord, loving Savior, lead me to hear your love in the silence and sense your will in the moments when you are mute. Amen.

Try This
At the end of day ask, "Lord what would you have me

know; what would you have me do?" Then listen for his still, small voice to tell you.

Signs of Jesus' Coming

When these things begin to take place, stand up and lift up your heads, because your redemption is drawing near. Luke 21:28

What things? You'd be surprised. It's a devastating catalog of crises and convulsion Jesus is talking about in Luke 21: ruthless forces playing havoc with the dreams of people, nation digging in against nation, famine, earthquake, persecution, the sea roaring and "men's hearts failing them for fear" (Luke 21:26, KJV). I should say. That's as timely a catalog as a person could come up with. The ink is still wet on that description. When all these things begin to happen, the very next time headlines tell you how violent hands have snuffed out the bright hope of this family or that set of parents, the next news cast about revolutions within and battles without somewhere on this globe, famine in Africa, earthquake in the West, hurricanes heading toward the East coast, despair and suicide because of economic conditions on Wall Street, I'll tell you what you do. Don't think about it. Jump into a golf cart. Organize a party. Push off the prospects as long as possible. There goes hope; here comes despair.

No! Not at all, not when Jesus Christ is in the picture. The same calamities and heartbreaks which sink the hope of some, stir our expectations and alert us to the entrance of an almighty and endlessly loving God upon the scene. Stand up; look around. Your redemption is hovering out there and coming closer. When your life is dark and you can't see the road in front of your feet, when the terror of the night becomes real and you're all bent over under a load of disappointment, stand up. Look around. Redemption is coming close. Jesus is there and his answers are pending.

Prayer

King of grace and Lord of glory, my hope is in your drawing near, and my renewal is in the promise of your coming. Alone I am hopeless, and by myself I am lost. But you are with me, your presence is my comfort. Amen.

Try This

Take two of your heaviest burdens and look at each in the light of the knowledge that Jesus is coming, is just beyond the next turn of life. Stand up. Look around. Your troubles tell you he is coming near.

Drop Anchor—1

They dropped four anchors from the stern and prayed for daylight. Acts 27:29

Does that sound familiar? When things have gotten that bad, have you ever done what you could and then prayed for the day? At a time like that, look to your anchors. They're all you have. If you want to know someone, really know him, find out what his anchors are. When there is nothing more a person can do, what is at the other end of the line to which he clings, while he prays, or she, for daylight?

"We have . . . hope as an anchor . . . " says the epistle to the Hebrews (Heb. 6:19). That's one anchor you can throw over the stern as you pray earnestly for some light at the end of the tunnel.

There was a day when good folks hoped, for God's sake and their own, that they might get in the good graces of the Almighty by doing good and thinking clean, going to church and contributing to the fund for the homeless and displaced. So they did, and then sat back and yearned for daylight. But the anchor kept slipping. It just wouldn't take hold. No matter how much they did or how well they did it, the darkness deepened. You just couldn't count on being good.

Then came St. Paul and shocked everybody by letting in the daylight: "May the God of hope fill you with all joy and peace" (Rom. 15:13). The God of hope, the God who creates hope, the God who is the "reason for the hope that is in us," he will hold your keel to the wind and usher in the day.

We're talking real anchors here. To be able to stake your future, not on what you do for God but on what he does for you in Jesus, on Calvary, and in Joseph's lovely garden, by living and dying and rising again for you and in your place, that is something to hold you when you can't do anything for yourself anymore.

Prayer

Help me, O God of my salvation, to make Jesus my hope, to hold my soul while darkness deepens 'round me. Amen.

Try This

At the end of the day, decide simply, and in so many words, to put your hope for your future in Jesus and go to sleep, confident that that anchor will see you through until daylight comes.

Drop Anchor—2

They dropped four anchors from the stern and prayed for daylight. Acts 27:29

Hope is an anchor. So is prayer. It doesn't take a superior IQ to fathom how prayer serves to steady the soul in rough seas. It's the Christian way in every storm, to bring God into it and undergird life with the love of heaven. "At last," cried an old saint in a moment of victory, "I have made firm my staggering soul." Prayer does that. It steadies the nerves. It raises our souls to levels where the headwinds of life are calmer. It makes us sure, as nothing else can, that God is our refuge and strength.

There was a day when going to God in prayer was a little like trying to get an appointment with the president of the United States. The way was pretty well blocked by ordained receptionists and ecclesiastical secretaries, and in the end someone always ended up delivering your message for you. You had to go through channels.

But each of us is a priest in his own right. Oh, not a certified, ecclesiastically-appointed, name-on-the-roster reverend, maybe, but priest enough to walk unannounced into the throne room and start talking. The "priesthood of believers" it's called by theologians who like to write essays about it. God is not quite so academic. "Come on in," is his way of putting it.

We have become accustomed to our privileges as

priests of God, so accustomed we fail often to exercise those privileges. Why not use this privilege of priesthood by walking in on God right now. Talk to him, and listen; that's always part of it. It's the kind of anchor which helps immensely to swing keel to the current while you look for daylight.

Prayer

I lift my hands and heart and voice to you, O Lord of life and heaven, and seek my peace in this privilege of prayer. Amen.

Try This

Design, on paper perhaps, a week's worth of daily prayers and use them at the close of day, for seven days. Then watch how the dawn comes and daylight with it. At the end of the exercise ask yourself if, and then how, prayer has steadied you and been an anchor for your soul.

Drop Anchor—3

They dropped four anchors from the stern and prayed for daylight. Acts 27:29

What do you think of this for an anchor for your soul: the Bible? Theologians like to point to the Reformation and say that the restoration of the Bible into the hands of common folks is one great gift of that Reformation to our times. And it is. But not always in the way we think. We conjure up visions of pre-Reformation days and cluck about the fact that the Bible was chained to reading tables.

We like to shake our heads over the way the church contrived to keep the good book out of common hands. Bibles, of course, were priceless things. You would have chained yours to the end table, too, or kept it in a vault if you had lived then. The contribution of the Reformation as it pertains to the Holy Bible was not about that.

The contribution of the Reformation as pertains to the Bible is that it freed it up to take its proper place in our lives. (And when we fail to give it such, we're just as guilty as history vis-a-vis the Bible.)

Young Johnny has been told by his parents to lead a chaste and decent life. The teacher in his social ethics class hands out contraceptives free of charge. There's a mixed message here. Who should he believe and what instruction should he follow? It's a puzzlement, in the words of the King of Siam. When God's word says one thing and society another, confusion rises in the Christian heart. Such confusion offers no safe haven, no comfort, and no anchor for the Christian soul. What to believe? Which to follow? But the Bible is our sole authority, our soul authority, our anchor. It isn't just the word; it's the last word. It's the Word of God.

Prayer

To your words, dear Lord, I commend my life, for guidance, for enlightenment, and for direction. Amen.

Try this

Find a passage in the Bible to give direction to our judgment with reference to the following: litigation; income tax reporting; euthanasia; abortion; capital punishment.

Drop Anchor—4

They dropped four anchors from the stern and prayed for daylight. Acts 27:29

Hope; prayer; Bible. Now Jesus Christ himself, none other. Is there any anchor for our souls like the love of God which you find in Jesus? We pray for the daylight, the moment when we see God as he is, when we stand toe to toe with the one who gave himself for our sins and died so that we may live forever. Nothing can hold us, no one can cradle us, like this one, while we long and wait and wish for the day. Jesus, on the cross, is our sure, unfailing anchor keeping us safe and holding us steady through the storms which sweep over us just by reason of our being alive.

At the center of our lives stands Christ. "On Christ, the solid rock I stand. All other ground is sinking sand." The Scripture is full of these pictures which set out to assure us that Jesus is refuge and Jesus is strength. In the Old Testament book of Isaiah you come across a graphic phrase which is a perfect description of Jesus—"the shadow of a great rock in a thirsty land" (Is. 32:2). For some of us who live near the mighty deserts of our land, these words come alive as a representation of our Savior. Out there in those barren expanses with inversion layers and the dynamics of high-low pressure weather patterns, the desert winds get a chance to pick up force and speed and whistle across the sandy hills carrying the stinging sand and dried sage with a force which can hurt and blind and do damage, indeed. There is nothing more comforting, if you're standing behind it, or leaning against it, than a mighty rock behind which to take refuge. The desert is a dreary, weary land, baking away and constantly moving and groaning and shrieking across the flats and down the hills. In such a land, a strong rock is the best refuge there is. Jesus is our anchor while we wait for daylight. He is our "strong rock in a weary land."

Prayer

Ah, dearest Jesus, let me hide myself in you. Keep me as the storms scream round me. Save me 'til I see the day. Amen.

Try This

Take the two things which most trouble you, which frighten you most, and ask Jesus to hold you steady through them, hide you from them, and keep you safe until the light eases the fear.

The Personal Touch

And he took the children in his arms, put his hands on them and blessed them. Mark 10:16

It goes too far to suggest that Jesus at a distance is no help at all. After all, the whole world has been immensely blessed by his coming. People who don't know of him, even people who deny him and hold him at arms length, all people share in the benefits which Jesus with his radically different and "other-minded" way of looking at things has insinuated into the commerce of this world. But the real blessings come when you are gathered in his arms.

I don't remember where I came across it, but I once found an illustration which tells about some youngsters playing in the sand on the seashore. They spotted an artist painting a seascape, and one of the children said, "Paint us into the picture, mister." Here is a challenge for Christianity: paint us into the picture. Christianity has a great deal to offer: peace in the midst of turmoil, purpose when everybody seems to be losing his head or devoting himself to nothing greater than number one, forgiveness when you know you have been less than you ought to be. All this is for everyone in Jesus. But it is so remote, so far removed, so church-like.

What have these to do with you? Listen! These things begin to live and move and have real being when you and I are in the picture. You and I need peace and purpose and forgiveness. The echoes of that need have sounded in the councils of our God. God has addressed an answer to our need: A decree went out from Caesar Augustus; a baby was born in Bethlehem; Jesus came to live and die for you. The Christian proclamation isn't about something that happened long ago and far away. It talks about something which reaches out to lay its grip on you and give you peace and purpose and forgiveness today. When you snuggle in his arms, that close, and he puts his hands on you, then he will shower you with his blessings.

Prayer

Move me into your picture, Lord, that I may have your blessing. Amen.

Try This

Read Luke 23:13–56 again and again, each time taking the place of the characters you find there: the multitude, Pilate, Simon, the malefactors, Joseph, the women. Get yourself into the picture.

Music Out of Sour Notes

I, Paul, the prisoner of Christ . . . . Ephesians 3:1

Actually, Paul was the prisoner of Nero. He was chained for safekeeping by the ankle to a burly Roman legionnaire in jail. But St. Paul had a way of looking at life which eyed every situation for the opportunity it provided. And here, as he saw it, was a captive audience chained down and handy every time he wanted to talk about the love of Christ. It was one of the ways, as another has put it, which Paul had of "turning calamity into a blessing," and twisting hard realities into magnificent opportunities.

If we could do that with our life it would remove all the gloom and self- pity we sometimes feel as we get older, and have us eager to get our feet over the side of the bed each morning. Heaven knows, and so do we, that there are plenty of things happening to us right now which most of us would catalog as troubles. To be able to take those and turn them around, twist them, see in them a new dawn and an opportunity, that would be quite an asset. Well, it's a big claim, but we claim it just the same: the ability to make music out of sour notes is a Christian specialty.

One of the things that impressed the ancient world about the young Christian church was the way in which its people faced with joy and eagerness the persecutions which were thrown at them. Far from being cowed by them and driven into full retreat, Christian people, just ordinary Christian people, turned their faces to the iron gates which led to the arena and with a whispered word of prayer faced off with lions. One of the things which impresses the world in which we live is the way Christians, just ordinary Christian people, lay hold of the hard facts of life and twist them into glorious opportunities to do good and show mercy and walk humbly with their God.

Prayer

Lord of my life, keep me from self-pity and show me how to use the things that happen in my daily walk to serve you and your cause. Amen.

Try this

Review yesterday. What were the things that made you feel sorry for yourself? How could you have used them for Christ's sake? With God's help, face today determined to turn every trouble into an opportunity to do his will and make Christ's kingdom come.

Prayer Really Helps

Is any one of you in trouble? He should pray. James 5:13

Yeah, yeah! People are always saying that. What earthly good will prayer do? Maybe that's it: no earthly good; just some ethereal, heaven-oriented, out-of-this-world, mysterious benefit. Do you have trouble? Maybe it's just a general weariness or hopeless feeling that's laid hold of you? Frustration, depression have this way of spoiling your day? Rainy days and Mondays get you down? Well, I, too, suggest you pray, and I'd like to tell you how prayer helps.

First of all, when you take your needs to God in prayer

you are going to set them in their right perspective. We're too near our troubles to assess their true importance. We have to stand back, the way you do in prayer, into the healing presence of God to get our proportions straight. In prayer we look at problems from the perspective of God and see their real significance, or insignificance. Next, prayer helps us bring our wills into line with God's. God says, "Do this." "But," says our will, "I want to do that." In prayer we take our wills and deliberately say, "Not my will, but thine be done." We say "no" to self and "yes" to God. We put our wills under God's command.

Finally, and this is most important, prayer connects us with the very power of God. Life is beyond most of us, and we all have days when we aren't up to it. In prayer we tie in to God and his power, and back down the line comes the power of God himself, flowing into our lives, making us adequate again.

Got trouble? Pray. It really works.

Prayer
Almighty Lord, whose throne is in heaven and whose footstool is the earth, what a privilege is ours that we may cast all our cares on you who cares for us! Lord, hear my own prayer in trouble and in peace, in season and out of season, for Jesus' sake. Amen.

Try This
Take one thing which troubles and lay it before Jesus with these words: Teach me the real significance or insignificance of this, my trouble. Teach me to do your will, not mine, as regards my trouble. Give me your strength to do your will in the face of my trouble.

Part of the Solution

Now my heart is troubled, and what shall I say?
John 12:27

If you don't mind a bit of advice, when you are in the presence of somebody who's got real trouble on his hands, you're often best off if you don't say anything. And so is he. So often people on the outside looking in add to the burden with some all embracing glibness about the "nobility of pain," or with the observation that "it could be worse." All that may be true enough, but the plain fact is the one in trouble doesn't need an explanation as much as he needs your hand under his arm, and whatever help you can give him. I think that's why you search the Bible in vain for answers to the question, why. Job's friends took turns explaining the calamities which had befallen him. And inevitably their answers added to his feelings of guilt, or his doubts about God's good intentions. Some help that was. But God didn't give Job answers to the question, why. He never does. He rephrases the question. He tells you how to stand up under the weight of whatever it is that bows your back. His answer tells you how.

And unlike the rest of us, his answer always tells you his part in the solution. Try that once, when someone you know is face-to-face with tragedy. Tell him what you're going to do to help him bear it.

In literature you come upon the picture of a woman who has met a sudden sorrow. "I wish I had never been created," she exclaims. And another answers, "You aren't, yet. You're being created, and this sorrow is part of the process." That's true, but only afterwards does that become apparent. Meanwhile, you take the troubled hand in yours, together you put your hands in Christ's, and then together you walk the treacherous path or live with the thorn.

Prayer

Man of sorrows, help me help others in any trouble with the same help which you give me in mine. Amen.

Try This

Pick two friends and identify what burdens each might have. Ask yourself how you might be of help: two things specifically, for each. Pray for each of them and then do what you have determined you can do to help. This week.

A Long, Long Trail A'Winding

They will soar on wings like eagles; they will run and not grow weary, they will walk and not be faint.
Isaiah 40:31

Most of the goals we set for ourselves in life are reached by putting one foot in front of the other, again and again, at a walk. Dart, dash, soar, and hurtle are favorite verbs in today's world. But for achievement, for fulfillment, for ultimate victory, it takes a pedestrian pace and a whole lot of what we are wont to describe as common drudgery.

A straight line may be the shortest distance between two points, but it is not necessarily the best road to travel. There is this need to fill up all the places on the way. For that you need time. That's why God led the children of Israel through the book of Exodus in circles. They weren't ready for the promised land. If they had been led there directly, they would have been slaves still, precisely as they were in Egypt. They needed what you could get by going "through the way of the wilderness" (Ex. 13:18, KJV). It was a long, slow walk, which would eat up forty years of their lives, but when they got there they'd be ready, ready to be the people of God.

There is a good reason why Isaiah puts on the brakes as he winds up this rhapsody in chapter 40. We exult to hear him talk of soaring flights and headlong dashes. But must he slow it all down to a walk at the end? "They will walk and not be faint." These bursts of enthusiasm and sudden gusts of energy which mark so much of the youthful journey with Jesus are well and good. Young people tend, after all, to measure life by its magnificent moments. But the walk of life goes on mile after mile, across long, flat, dreary plains, and over high, challenging mountains, tough going and slow. "They will walk and not faint."

There are advantages to senior status. One of them is a quiet understanding born of personal experience, that the goals of life, even eternal life, are achieved at a walk.

Prayer

Guide, direct, and empower my steps, dear Lord, 'til I am safely home. Amen.

Try This

Divide your life's history into segments: childhood, youth, early adulthood, middle age, senior status. Remind yourself how "daily" all the stages of your life have been. Look up Hebrews 10:23. Thank God that through all the long walk of your life, God has been a faithful God who has not left you or forsaken you.

Bright and Shining Hours

I can do everything through him who gives me strength. Philippians 4:13

Have you noticed that those moments which seem bleakest in the long run often turn out to be the bright and shining hours of our lives? I don't know why that should be, unless it's because the devil always overplays his hand. He did it on Calvary, pushed things too far, and God turned it into the supreme moment of history, with Satan crushed forever. Maybe the good that is in us, the good which God puts there, comes out best under pressure. At any rate, you can read it on every page of history: Stephen in the stone pit, Paul in prison, Daniel in the lion's den. Well, you have your own history and have discovered yourself how it works.

That ought to provide you with a sense of confidence as you face your future. Quit defending yourself. Go on the offensive. If your primary activity is trying not to get hurt too badly, as it is for so many in this world, God will have gotten out so far ahead of you, you are apt to be left utterly exposed. Take the offensive. Start marching through thick and thin for Jesus, and in his name, and you will find that you're not "without God in this world." When you come to some place which you truly dread, God is there first, ahead of you, waiting, watching, mounting guard. You, especially you, child of God, can hardly play the coward's part when God has you surrounded behind and before, and underneath are his everlasting arms.

Everyday on the way to work you can read a half

dozen bumper stickers which declare, "Have a happy day!" That's nice, I guess. But I keep thinking when a Christian opens his mouth, something stronger ought to come out—something like, "Everything through him who gives me strength."

Prayer

Triumphant, Triune God, my comfort and my strength are in your promise to be with me to the end of time. With you at hand to bless there is no moment I cannot face in triumph. Amen.

Try This

Read the Old Testament book of Daniel. Ask how God's presence made Daniel equal to his troubles.

Timely Eulogies

Speak well of him, and explain everything in the kindest way. Explanation to the eighth commandment, Luther's Small Catechism

This has been a summer for funerals. Especially for us who live under the shadow of that modern euphemism, "seniors," going off to "bury our dead" is a common enough activity. Have you noticed our habit of trotting out and airing a person's strong points and positive contributions after the fact of his or her final triumph, when we simply did not take the pains to do it before? We're prone during a person's lifetime on this earth to isolate and dissect and underscore our friend's weaknesses and shortcomings.

We've got it upside down and backwards. It would

seem more productive and helpful, I should think, to let go with a few complimentary eulogies while a person can still benefit from them. If we approach each other with the same respect and honor and preference in our daily commerce with each other that we are wont to haul front and center as we gather to pay our "final respects," we'd go a long way toward making the most of people's gifts and contributions. At least such eulogy would come at a time when a person can do something with it.

We will not have each other always, you and I, you and yours. God has given each of us our circle of friends and fellow humans. And all of us possess our own strengths and weaknesses. It seems reasonable and wise that, while life shall last, we maximize our companions' strengths and minimize their weaknesses. That's good for them and us, and just makes common sense. At their funerals, if you are so inclined, then you can remind yourself and everyone else of their inadequacies. It won't much matter then. And you won't feel so intent on doing it. Meanwhile, speak well of them, whoever they are, and put the best construction on everything.

Prayer

Help me, my Lord and Master, make the most of the gifts which you have given to the people with whom I live and move and have my being. And help me to overlook, or even better, to help them at the point of their weaknesses, for everybody's good and in obedience to your will. Amen.

Try This

Pick two friends. Assess their strengths and compliment them. Help them use their abilities to good advantage. And purposely ignore their weaknesses.

❖

Here He Comes Again

Speak tenderly to Jerusalem. Isaiah 40:2

The Battle Hymn of the Republic talks about the "glory of the coming of the Lord." Any time our Lord comes upon the scene it is glorious, I should say. The very notion that a great arrival is pending sends shivers up the spine. Just think, something magnificent is being gotten ready up there, and some day soon, sooner than you think, if the Bible is to be believed, it will burst upon the human scene. I love the way the Christian Gospel catches its breath and shouts out loud, "Here he comes again."

It's not just the glory, but the comfort of it which strikes you. We all have problems, and life is terribly much harder for some, than any who observe them can imagine. But sometimes, through the darkness, shines a light, and the troubled heart grows calm again. "Be still my soul. God will surely come."

A great preacher from an earlier era said, "If I had my ministry to live over again, I would strike the note of comfort far more often than I did." Has it ever occurred to you how committed Jesus is to giving comfort? Do you think he did all those miracles simply to impress those who were looking on? I think he did them out of compassion for those before him in their need. He didn't die to prove something. He died to be something, a savior; he died to save us all. We are caught in the sins that spoil our lives and trouble our memories, and temptations which after all these years we still can't seem to break, and wild regrets for past mistakes. Jesus sees that and instinctively reaches out to one and then another, and lets them nail him, arms stretched out like that, to the cross, because he wants to be our comforter.

Soon Christ will come again. And when he comes he will have words of comfort for you. God knows we need them. "Speak tenderly to Jerusalem," the Old Testament scribe enjoined. Tenderly, because he comes again, to comfort and console us.

Prayer

Hold me, Savior, in your tender arms and hurry the day when you will come again to speak your tender words of forgiveness. Amen.

Try This

Apply Christ's tender words, "Your sins will I remember no more," to the memory of the one most troubling, nagging sin you have ever committed.

How to Keep Cool When the Heat's On

You did not choose me, but I chose you and appointed you to go and bear fruit. John 15:16

Age brings with it its own advantages. One of them is a subtle relaxing of the pressures we are under, just by reason of being alive. Still, while the pressure cooker may be easing, chances are better than even that, for many of us, the heat is still on.

At one time, when I would complain about the incessant pressures under which I found myself, a good friend, coworker actually, would suggest, borrowing the words of

Harry S. Truman, "If you can't stand the heat, get out of the kitchen." In fact, he would repeat that so frequently, it built up some pressure all its own just listening to him say it.

There are better ways to "beat the heat," you know, ways to stay cool in the middle of your pressure pot. One way is to remember to whom you, as a child of God, are responsible. I refer to Jesus. He is the one, the one and only, when all is said and done, to whom you are responsible. Half our pressures root in trying to please everybody. But Jesus is not nearly so hard to please as people are. What, after all, does he require? Simply that you be found faithful. People, family, friends, the boss, all insist that you succeed. Jesus asks simply that you try, faithfully, with everything you've got.

Here's another way to keep cool. Recall that Jesus thinks you are the right man or woman for the job, whatever it is. He sent his Son to enlist you in his service. He sent his Spirit to set up housekeeping in your heart. He did all this because he sees some promise in you, some confidence that you are right for the tasks he wants you to do. He chose you, and not the other way around.

Add them up: they spell cool in the heat of all your pressures.

Prayer

Remind me, O my God, that for all my sins and weaknesses, you have chosen me to be your own, to serve you in everlasting righteousness, innocence, and blessedness. Amen.

Try This

Focus on the one overriding hot spot in your life. Tell yourself that God chose you to face it and work through it because he has judged that you are right for the job. Do your best. If you come out winner, thank God. If you don't, thank God anyhow and move right on.

Amazing Grace

I have loved you with an everlasting love. Jeremiah 31:3

That sentence means so very much more than we imagine. "I have loved you," so speaks God. But what is God to us? Not half of what he was to the man who first set these words to paper. He was thinking, take my word for it, of the one who becomes whatever it is you need. If you need a brother, God becomes your brother. If it is power you have to have, God is power. Forgiveness? God is our forgiver. There may be no earthly reason why God should love us, but there is plenty of reason in heaven. God is by nature what we need, and we need love. If we were a thousand times worse than we are, and it's hard to imagine us much worse than we are, God would love us, because of what he is. "I have loved you."

"With an everlasting love." The commentaries give a neat twist to these words. Love that goes beyond the vanishing point, that's what they say that means. The end of God's love is forever beyond the horizon. Climb up on Calvary and God's love towers over you. Climb earth's highest mountain. God's love is higher still. Burrow down until there is nothing left beneath. Still God's love is under you to hold you.

"I have loved you with an everlasting love." The gender is feminine. We forever want to talk about the fatherhood of God. Motherhood is more like it. And I don't mean that in any modern, liberated sense. "I, have loved you with a beyond-the-vanishing point mother love." That's what it means. I, who always become whatever it is you need, have mother-loved you because I must, with a tender concern which, wherever you are, covers so high above you and so far around you and so deep beneath you that its limits extend beyond your horizon, and run right out of sight.

Prayer

Great Redeemer, strong to save, your grace reaches out to cover all my sins, and your love satisfies all my needs. How lavish you are to bring to my poverty more than I can ever use. To your name be glory, you who are what it is that I require. Amen.

Try This

List in your mind the five things you need the most. Then conceptualize how God becomes the answer to those needs.

So This Is God

The Word became flesh and made his dwelling among us. John 1:14

Here is an over-worked illustration, but it still has its points. A missionary's son came to America to get an education. On his desk he kept his father's picture. Shortly before Christmas one of his professors visited him in his room and asked him what he wanted most for Christmas. The student answered, "I want my father to step out of that frame." The gospels are the story of God stepping out of the frame of eternity to reveal himself to us in Jesus.

I remember taking part in a lively conversation about religion in which the participants included several skeptics. One of them challenged a reference I had made to God using the pronoun "him." "How do you know God is 'he'? How can you be sure? Maybe God is just an idea. Maybe God is a figment of human imagination. How do you know what God is?" To that question, Christmas is the answer. In Jesus of Bethlehem, God "became flesh and made his dwelling among us" where we could get to know a lot about him. Granted what we don't know about God is considerably more than we know. But we know enough to take comfort in his love and his forgiveness. In Jesus, God became a known God, at least that much of him.

We smile fondly at that little baby in a manger and respond each year to the lovely sentiment of Christmas. We love the story about angels and wise men and delight in singing Christmas carols. But when you get right to the center of it, the strength and grip of Christmas is this: you can look at Jesus, born quietly in Bethlehem "when half spent was the night," and only shepherds working the night shift, or revelers cooking up a morning headache, or old men enduring a bout of gout, were up and around, and you can say, "So this is God."

Prayer

O Dayspring from on high, Babe of Bethlehem, in you I have come to know the love and the compassion of my God. Praise be to you, Sun of Righteousness, risen with healing in your wings. Amen.

Ponder Jesus. List three of his obvious attributes. What does it mean to you today, that these are the attributes of God?

Who Needs the Church?

Let us not give up meeting together, as some are in the habit of doing, but let us encourage one another.
Hebrews 10:25

There was a fellow who claimed he was a Christian, but didn't have to go to church. Whenever the local minister invited him to join the faithful in their worship, he would answer, "I am a good Christian and I do not need the church." Evidently he has a lot of company.

One cold, wintry day, that minister called on the fellow in his home and was immediately invited to warm himself by the fire. The man was certain the minister would invite him to church, and stood poised to give out his standard answer, "I am a good Christian and I don't need the church." Instead, however, the minister said nothing, but took the chair he was offered. After gazing at the flames for a little, he took one glowing ember from the fire and set it off by itself to the side. Slowly at first, then quickly, the ember cooled until at last it lost its light and warmth altogether. The minister rose and left.

I'd like to have the smarts to do something dramatic and effective like that. A person could come closer to it, I suppose, if he didn't forever insist on verbalizing every lesson he set out to teach. Without a word that minister got his point across: embers burn bright when they burn together, but separated, tend to cool and die. Christians burn bright and strong together. In isolation they can cool, and even die out totally.

Prayer

Lord of the church, who has set the solitary in families to nourish and comfort the faithful, make strong the tie that binds me to my fellow-Christians. Impress upon my consciousness my need for those with whom I share my Christian faith, and my need to nourish them in theirs. Amen.

Try This

Pick three fellow Christians to whom you will say a word of thanks that they are fellow Christians and that, being so, they foster and make strong your Christian life and faith.

The Future Is in God's Hands

Even to your old age . . . I . . . will sustain you. I have made you and I will carry you. Isaiah 46:4

Thus saith the Lord, and we shouldn't forget it. People who qualify for senior rates by and large have little confidence in the future of this old world. Granted we didn't do much of a job at the helm of humanity's ship while it was our turn, and we do seem to have presided over a wholesale abandoning in our lifetime of all that is chaste and decent. When you take a hard, long look at the movers and shakers of the next generation, it prompts you to shake the head and cluck the tongue and raise the eyebrow. What are our children going to face in the early and mid-twenty-first century, and how will they manage? But God reminds us, and we take comfort from it, "I have made you and I will carry you."

It's the same old reminder to keep our hands off. It isn't just that we have done a less than creditable job in our own immediate past. It's that it isn't our job in the first place, directing the course of this world. It isn't on your shoulders or mine. Oh, we have responsibilities all right. God expects us to be faithful. He has bought us with a price; we are his, and that means obedience and following in his steps. But there is an overwhelming arrogance about our despair for our children and the future of God's world. Remember, God is this world's creator, and he has not left it nor forsaken it.

The worshippers of Baal, 600 or so years before the birth of Jesus, were forever having to pick up their idols and cart them off for safe-keeping whenever the enemy threatened. They had to take care of their gods instead of their gods taking care of them. There are religions which are little more than a burden, dead weight, a load to carry. But God, our God, insists, "Even to your old age I will sustain you. I have made you and I will carry you."

Prayer

Blessed Maker and Redeemer, assure me and comfort me that what you have begun you will perfect. As you have sustained me to old age, sustain those faithful still to come. Into your hands I commend my children and theirs and everyone, indeed, until you close this world's book of life. Amen.

Try This

Identify three cataclysmic events in history which God has used to do his will and make his kingdom come.

Believing Is Better

[You] *believe in God, believe also in me.* John 14:1, KJV

There isn't much prospect in unbelief. I would be inclined, if I were an unbeliever, to begin to doubt my doubts. One trouble with the road of unbelief is that there is no prospect but ultimate zilch, zero, nothing. No support for your best, and no reason to suppose your best is any better than the worst. No God whose purpose is unfolding, no Christ to raise up bleeding hands to save us all; no kingdom to serve with the confidence that his is the kingdom, and the power, and the glory, forever and ever. Like a vine which can climb no higher than the trellis it twists around, a human life can climb no higher than the scaffold of its faith. Unbelief isn't a big enough trellis.

Christian belief, on the other hand, affirms that when we look at Jesus Christ, we see what is behind it all—the love God has for his creatures, and the purpose he pursues to make them his sons and daughters. It says we have seen "the glory of God in the face of Christ" (2 Cor. 4:6).

You choose either God, the Father of our Lord Jesus Christ, or you choose nothing. Well, that isn't just right either. You might choose nothing, that's a possibility. But you won't choose God and his Son, Jesus. He has chosen you. He has made you his own to live under him in his kingdom. You can be eternally thankful he did.

George Bernard Shaw once claimed, "There was only one Christian, and we crucified him." He meant there was only one who lived like a Christian. And there he has a point. But Christianity isn't how you live. It is whose you are: You belong to God and his Son, Jesus. That is a belief which affords real prospects, for now and forever.

Prayer

By your choice I am yours, dear Savior. What desolation had you not won me, a lost and condemned creature, and planted faith in my heart. To your name I sing my praise. Amen.

Try This

Review the Apostles' Creed, phrase by phrase. Imagine your life if you did not believe the precepts articulated there. Then pray, Lord, I believe; help thou my unbelief.

In the Time That's Left

Making the most of every opportunity. Ephesians 5:16

"Redeeming the time," says the King James Version. Bible translations are fascinating, especially by comparison. In the original, these words read something like this: "buying up for yourselves the seasonable time." One translation of that talks about what we ought to do (KJV), the other (NIV) how we ought to do it. Both have a contribution to make.

It is certainly appropriate, especially for those of us for whom time is becoming a cherished commodity, to buy up as much as we can, make the most of it, and treat it as the precious thing it is. Can you remember when you were in the third grade? You slouched there with your cheek in your hand and watched the sun make little patterns in slow motion on the dust particles floating in the air. Time dragged. You wondered if recess, or the end of the school day would ever come. Not anymore. Three unexacting exercises like going to the bank, the post office, and the gas station consume the entire morning. Time is on an accelerating scale. The longer you live, the faster it goes. Did Einstein figure that into his theoretic formulas, I wonder? It makes you want to grab hold of it, time, snatch it from its headlong hurtle, save it, keep it, redeem it, if you can.

You can; at least the Bible says so. The way to do it is to make the most of every opportunity. Looking back on life you can spot the moments when by reason of forgetfulness or indolence or thoughtlessness you let the golden moment "pass you by." It didn't seem to matter. Tomorrow was another day. "I'll catch it next time." But for many of us, could be for all of us, the chances will not always come. We will not have each other always. You had planned to say "thank you" or "I'm sorry" or "I love you." Is there an old friend you owe a note, or an old enemy you owe an apology? Is God maintaining someone on the edge of health so that you can tell him about Jesus? Tomorrow may be too late. Today. Redeem the time. Make the most of your opportunities, every one of them.

Prayer
Help me fill what time remains to me, my God, with opportunities seized and victories won. Amen.

Try This

Determine three things you have so far left undone that you will do today. Then do them.

Our Times Are in God's Hands

The Lord gave and the Lord has taken away; may the name of the Lord be praised. Job 1:21

A television news show interviewed this fellow in Los Angeles who announced that he had aided, abetted, and attended the suicides of over twenty of his friends. They were all in the latter throes of the processes of AIDs, and their deaths seemed to be inevitable. The idea of dying the death which attends that dread disease seemed undignified to the dying and to this self-appointed assistant to death. He was so sure of himself that he took some pride in his record of achievement. There was a hush and an aura which surrounded his description of his "ministry." You'd think, at least he would, that *he* was God.

There are days for some when death seems sweet release and the end is a doorway to final victory. St. Paul had this constant thrill at the thought of "departing." It seemed to him to be "better by far" (Phil. 1:23). But he never hurried it, never took it all in his hands, twisted it, or insisted "my will be done." No matter what your life circumstance, God is not suddenly asleep or disinterested. He knows your coming and your going. He's on top of it. His will—the mystery of his plan, the purpose of his directing, no matter the sorrow or pain—must be done. Jesus saw it, and the martyrs. God has given; He will take away.

When things get bad for one we know and love, is this really the best we can do for him—lay out the tools of his own demise and hold his hand as he takes his life? Or can we comfort him with the reminder that we are in God's hands, and he is the very God who has gone to prepare a place for us, and will come again to take us to himself in heaven? An arm around the shoulder, holding the hand of a brother or sister, surely, as God comes to take a loved one to himself—that's ministry.

Prayer

Thy will, dear Lord, be done. Where that will is sweet and gentle, I rest my soul in you. When that will is difficult and rigorous, I trust your purpose and your victory, and mine. Amen.

Try This

Each evening say, "Thy will be done. Such time as I have is in God's hands. I will make the most of it for Jesus' sake."

He's on His Way

The Lord is near. Philippians 4:5

I love Advent.

Nowadays you call up from the airport to say you're passing through; how about lunch. In former days you wrote to say that you were coming. Writing letters is just one of the niceties of courtesy which is getting lost between the cracks which are appearing in the fabric of the jet age. Advent is God sending word ahead that he is coming.

When I was a boy the best part of Christmas came in the days just before it—the anticipation, the hope, the little lists, and the waiting. Granted, we didn't start in the middle of October the way department stores do. But that concentration into three weeks plus in December was almost as good as Christmas Day itself.

It's awfully hard to fit Advent onto the law side of the ledger. Oh, I know there's all this about repentance and "make straight the way." But even on our knees, heads all bowed down and muttering "Father, forgive me," the excitement is there. Jesus is coming. And what you really feel, all through Advent, inside, is the same thing which makes youngsters elbow each other and suppress their giggles during high and holy moments. If we ever let ourselves go, we will discover that Advent has more than one foot on the Gospel side, and the announcement that Christ is coming, not just for lunch on the way through, or to visit, but to stay and take over, is the "glad tidings of great joy" already.

When Advent comes (if you want to wait that long) go ahead and laugh. It certainly won't disturb any pious pretense in me. I'll understand perfectly. Jesus is coming. Here's an elbow in the ribs. Our Savior is on the way.

Prayer

King of grace and Lord of glory, my hope is in your coming and my renewal is in the anticipation of your drawing near. Help me to live all year long in the glow of that promise. Amen.

Try This

Make a list of all the difficult things in your life which will disappear when Jesus comes, and of the good things which will occur when he does.

New Life

*Just as Christ was risen from the dead through the
glory of the Father, we too may live a new life.*
Romans 6:4

That's quite a promise. St. Paul always put it as
strongly as he could. New life, really! It was part of Paul's
Easter refrain.

A lengthy catalog of blessings is ours because of Easter. St. Paul, who delights in catalogs, authored an impres-
sive one under the general category of the upshot and result of Jesus' resurrection. Faith is ours, as opposed to unbelief; righteousness instead of sin; eternal life rather than
an everlasting grave; a new and glorious body for the aches
and pains we live with presently (1 Cor. 15:22). Because of
Jesus' resurrection, "we too may live a new life."

St. Paul gets down to brass tacks. Jesus died and all
your sins died with him (Rom. 4:25). The old you is
through. The eccentric, thoughtless, selfish sinner has
been crucified. In Christ, a new you rises on Easter morning and every morning, a holy, just, and loving you.

I guess all of us have earnestly wished at one time or
another for a second chance, for an opportunity to start all
over again. Easter is the announcement of another chance,
the opportunity to start all over again, with a clean slate.
But Easter is more. It is the announcement that this time
you can do it right. You are no longer destined for the same
old failures. "As Christ was risen . . . we too may live a new
life." What makes it possible? Jesus, the risen Jesus. He
takes up residence in our hearts and a whole new way of

living results. We live no longer for ourselves. We live for him, "who died for us and rose again."

Prayer

Risen and triumphant Savior, you have brought me a new day, a day which spells new life, a renewal day. I raise happy hands in tribute to you who gives me life, new life. You have made newness the hallmark of my days. Amen.

Try This

Identify three things which need renewal in your life. Remember because Jesus is risen, you, too, may have new life. What will your day be like if those three things are renewed? Now go and live this day in newness of life.

Happy, Happy

For the kingdom of God is . . . a matter of . . . joy in the Holy Spirit. Romans 14:1.

Certain features of Christianity are hallmarks. It is questionable whether Christianity, apart from them, is Christianity at all. Love is one such. "By this all men will know that you are my disciples, if you love one another" (John 13:35). Patience is another (Rom. 5:4, KJV). Diligence qualifies, according to St. Paul (2 Cor. 8:7, KJV). What do you think of this for a sign, a hallmark, of Christian faith? Joy. Joy in the Holy Ghost.

It isn't too terribly hard to follow the logic. When you consider the alternatives to faith, catalog all the things it means to have it, consider what a glorious inheritance is ours with the saints, you've got to feel pretty good about it all. It's when you look into your daily life, pick a Monday and put it under a microscope, remember how you go around calling it blue, that you wonder. Is joy the mark of your Christian faith? Do people look at you and say to themselves, "Something for sure is tickling him." There are sure signs that a person is a believer in Christ, special signatures of genuineness. Joy is one of them.

Prophets of gloom, take note. Dealers in dejection and purveyors of pessimism, get ready. Underscorers of all that's wrong, look alive. Anyone who has come to know God as he is revealed in Jesus Christ is in for a surge of cheer and elation which dispels the somber overcast. You can feel it well up inside at the very thought of God's predisposition to love you in Jesus. Christianity and a gloomy outlook are mutually exclusive.

Nothing is more counterfeit than the stereotype of a glum, rigid, legalistic person running around under the label, child of God. Ask St. Paul. "Joy in the Holy Ghost" is the way he puts it.

Prayer

Lord, let none look at me and think that being a child of God is gloom and constant, somber dullness. Instead let me shine with the joy of my salvation and glow with the warmth of my love for you. Amen.

Try This

Once each hour think of Jesus. Smile. Then be prepared to give a reason for the joy that is in you.

❖

Warm-up Time

Because you are lukewarm—neither hot nor cold—I am about to spit you out of my mouth. Revelation 3:16

One problem, out of several, which pesters whenever one reads the book of Revelation is the knowledge that there is a sentence coming at which we'd just as soon never have to arrive. It isn't simply that the language lacks polish. What raises our defenses already a page or two before we come to it is its utter appropriateness, the way it hews so close to our poor Christian bones. "Because you are lukewarm—neither hot nor cold—I am about to spit you out of my mouth."

That's not only true; it's tragic. That is why all the recent talk about renewal for the Christian church, equating it with an overhaul of structure, or democratizing the committee process, or resurrecting a sense of the importance of the local parish, just to mention three which I think are very important, is pretty foolish talk. What we need is not a new blueprint. We need a new drum. "Without enthusiasm," said J. Parker, "the church . . . is Vesuvius without fire, Niagara without water, and the firmament without the sun."

If you want to know the church's overriding need, ask yourself what is your overriding need. Is it not for a match to kindle the fires of faith and enthusiasm and wide-eyed wonder again? Athletes warm up. Engines warm up. How do Christians warm up? There is one for that precise purpose: the Holy Spirit. He can make a cold heart catch fire and a cool one renew its ardor. You'll find him in the white pages of your Bible.

Prayer

Where the flame of faith and the fire of Christian wonder, O Spirit of God, flicker and grow dim for me, teach me again the glory of your grace and fill me with amazement for the love which Christ has shown for me. Amen.

Try This

Compare the promise of the next three television ads you see with the promise of the Gospel. Which deserves the enthusiasm of the one who pitches them? Which affords real hope, new life, lasting benefit? Which do you choose?

The Law of Christ

Carry each other's burdens, and in this way you will fulfill the law of Christ. Galatians 6:2

Someone says, "I've got a problem," or " I need some help." Instinctively our reaction is one of referral. "Go see the pastor," we advise. "I'll give you the name of my doctor." "I know a really good psychologist." We see ourselves as a switching yard in human life. People or problems or challenges come our way, and we deftly hand them off to this clergyman or that committee or this agency. We all do it. It's a new role we play in life.

My mother, fifty, sixty years ago, would never have done that. Whatever it was I brought her way, whatever the problem I shared with her, my problem, immediately it was her problem too. I went to her with the confidence that she would feel some responsibility. She didn't even punt the trouble to my father, unless it was something which required his ultimate input too. It was always good to know that she was there, that whatever I brought to her, from that moment on, we were in this thing together.

Referring people to the specialist is okay, but not as a method for ducking responsibility. The process of passing along problems can lead us to think we have fulfilled our Christian responsibility once we have dumped it, whatever it is, into the ear of whomever we feel ought to do something about it.

It doesn't work that way. Not for the people of Christ. Each of us, under the tutelage of him who took all our troubles and problems upon himself, needs to develop a sense of responsibility. When a problem arises, it's a matter of what you can do about it. What part will you play in its solution?

Prayer

Help me, dearest Jesus, be my brother's brother, to put my shoulder to his need and my resources at his disposal. As you have taught by word and by the example of your life, so I would help to bear the burdens of those with whom I live and move and have my being. Amen.

Try This

When someone shares a burden, ask yourself and her or him if there is a legitimate role you can play in its solution.

Faithful to Our Convictions

The Lord forbid that I should give you the inherit-
ance of my fathers. 1 Kings 21:3

One reason, among others, I think the Bible was in-
spired for people in our day is that the writer of First Kings
included in his book the story of Naboth. He was the fellow, you may remember, who refused to give up his inheritance for no other reason than that he didn't think it was
right. He had a vineyard, a family parcel, which King Ahab
wanted to acquire. It was a friendly enough business dealing to begin with. You couldn't say the king wasn't being
fair: a better producing vineyard in exchange or a straight
cash deal. It was a real estate person's dream of an offer.
But Naboth kept remembering the rubric God had laid
down in Numbers 36:7, "Every Israelite shall keep the tribal
land inherited from his forefathers," and the straightfor-
ward directive of Leviticus 25:23, "The land must not be
sold permanently." "No," said Naboth, which is a rather
unique answer to give to a king, "the Lord forbid," which is
even more unique, especially in our day, as a reason.

Well, you can see the point as it regards us. There are
offers galore for us to trade in the strong religious convictions of our fathers in favor of modern, popular, vague reli-
giousness. A God of creation, a virgin whose son was the
offspring of God, a resurrected savior and a king who forgives sins, the notion that we have sins at all—the strong
suggestion is to give all this up and settle for the sweet-
ness and niceness and light which some think Christianity
is really about, anyhow. It comes with age, maybe, this

growing appreciation for the substance of what we have inherited from our fathers. What we need is the spirit of old Naboth, a spirit which is willing to say no, and to say it because it just isn't right. "The Lord forbid that I should give you the inheritance of my fathers."

Prayer

Make me strong, my Lord, in my convictions. What you have decreed, human wisdom cannot annul. To your truth I hold. Amen.

Try This:

Identify three basic Christian precepts at which modernism scoffs. What will your answer be to those who would have you relinquish your onetime commitment to these basics?

The Good News

You are to give him the name Jesus, because he will save his people from their sins. Matthew 1:21

St. Matthew editorializes, "Jesus . . . because he will save his people from their sins." Jesus delivers us from sin, something we can't accomplish for ourselves.

If the truth were told, most of us don't spend a lot of time worrying about our sins. The news of the Gospel doesn't seem half so good to us as it did to the angel choirs over Bethlehem's fields or St. Peter as he preached on Pentecost. Maybe if we took our sins more seriously, we'd thrill more to the news of their forgiveness.

Imagine waiting in a hospital bed to die. You've been

told the tumor is inoperable and the illness is terminal. You are disconsolate as you count the hours, when your doctor bursts in to announce, "We have just discovered a cure for what ails you." That would be good news, wouldn't it, the kind of news that brings tears to the eyes and prompts hurried phone calls and makes you want to break out in a chorus of "Amazing Grace"?

You're drifting, let us say, on a piece of flotsam in an open sea, ready to pack it in, let go, and drown. Suddenly there is a light, then a ship, and finally a rescue. That light, that ship, is good news. The scientist who discovered the cure, the captain who brought his ship alongside, are saviors. They have done for you what you couldn't do for yourself. Would you like some good news? Jesus the Savior, has come to do for you what you cannot do for yourself— to save you from your sin.

The Bible takes sin seriously. When you take a long, hard look at Jesus you can see the measure to which we have spoiled things, the distance we have fallen from the heights on which God intended us to live. But Jesus has reversed all that, forgiven, restored, and renewed us. That's good news.

Prayer

Nothing in life, heavenly Father, can match the wonder of the news that in Christ I am forgiven and my everlasting life is assured. Help me to glory in Christ's victory for me. Amen.

Try This

Ask yourself, if Christ had not come, had not died, were not risen, what would my life be like? What comfort would I know? What reason for joy, today, could I find? What purpose would be mine?

All in the Family

God sets the lonely in families. Psalm 68:6

Last week my grandson learned to tie his own shoes. The next day he called to report it. He was bubbling over with a sense of accomplishment. And I was bubbling too. I haven't felt so much fulfillment since I learned to use the word eclectic in a sentence. What is it that allows us so much gratification in the successes of someone we love?

Whatever it is, it is "meet, right, and salutary." We are social creatures by the design of God. He has made us family. We've been programmed by our Maker to ache when our "others" are hurt, and swell with proper pride when someone in the family, immediate or extended, comes upon success.

It cuts a couple of ways, of course. Failures have a way, too, of reaching out and affecting those who love us, even those who don't know or love us. Sin is social too; that's been made obvious in our day. (Grandparents have an advantage at this point. They can and do tie in with every positive accomplishment, every coup de maitre, of their grandchildren as if it were their own, and then abdicate, at least fade a little into the background, when the piper must be paid. To be a grandparent carries with it undeniable privileges in this regard, which God obviously allows as a sort of bonus to those who live long enough.)

The point is, no man is an island. We are, each of us, part of an endless march called human history. We are the human family. Life is like an orchestra. Nobody's part is unimportant. The French horn, along with everybody else, makes beautiful music when it's on key and spoils it for everybody when it isn't. There is something very basic about it when we find satisfaction in what our children's children are achieving. They are writing our future. They are contributing their chapter to our book of life. To swell up when the story reads well is not contrived. God made it to be that way.

Prayer

How earnestly I pray, O Lord, when I lay into your hands the lives and hearts and future of those whom I call family. Indeed dear Savior, watch over, guard, and protect the whole human family, and call all men to faith and, through their faith, to heaven. Amen.

Try This

Take pen in hand to tell your children and their children of your love for them, and pride in them, and let them know how they are on your heart and in your prayers.

Maximizing Potential

She did what she could. Mark 14:8

Here's a notion which may help you in your relationship with spouse or friend or fellow worker. It's what I call "maximizing people's potential."

Most of us, as the day goes by, do what we do best or what comes easiest, as opposed often to what needs doing most. If I have to choose between doing something distasteful, but necessary, and something I like to do, I have a lot of trouble not opting for what comes easiest and is apt to have the best results. We're all like that.

I've noticed members of Christian congregations grow impatient with people on the church staff because, while "he preaches very well," they say, he doesn't "give us any administrative leadership." Or, they complain, "She is an excellent teacher, but she doesn't sing in choir." Then a struggle ensues, feelings get hurt, and criticisms are rendered. No staff person is good at everything, and most staff persons tend to concentrate on what they do well. Actually, that tendency might well get the best out of them. It "maximizes their potential," so to speak.

I have this notion that one reason God placed us in this world at this time and place is to help maximize the potential of those with whom we relate. One way to do that is to encourage people to do what they do well, and assist them to cover the areas where their inclinations make them less than diligent. The suggestion is that we expect and encourage the people with whom we relate to do what they do well and happily, and fill in as best we can for them whatever gaps that leaves. After all, what does the Lord require? He requires that people do their best. Dare we require more?

Prayer
Soften all my criticism of others and cause me to help my fellows where their efforts leave some things undone, O God, you who expects only that we do our best. Amen.

Try This
Determine what you can do to make another's life most productive.

He Is Risen

Christ has indeed been raised from the dead.
1 Corinthians 15:20

According to a front page article in a major Western newspaper several years ago, it's just you and St. Paul and I who think so. According to that article, the traditional understanding of the resurrection is "out of step with the prevailing views of most prominent biblical scholars." I have a little trouble with that word "biblical" since it refers, in this case, to the very people whose approach to the Bible is to eliminate as much of it as possible, certainly anything that makes of Jesus "the Word made flesh" or claims that he "rose bodily from the dead." The phrase "unbiblical scholarship" commends itself.

But just as bothersome is the word "scholarship." It seems to me that a segment of intellectuals has pre-empted the word for itself, as if it has an exclusive right to it. Poets who rhapsodize over all that they have seen and heard, celebrators who compose psalms of praise about what they have been told, humble men and women who keep and ponder in their hearts all that has been revealed to them, are these not scholars, students, masters even, of all the Bible says?

We have a prophetic role to play in our day and age. If the intellectual elite have contrived to satisfy themselves, out of the ingenuity of their minds, to abandon the idea of the resurrection of Christ, then you and I must proclaim what we believe, and believe what God has told us, that Jesus is "my beloved Son," and "he is risen from the dead."

By the time another front page article on the subject appears, let's make sure we are exempt from any suggestion that today's "best minds" know better. After all, "If Christ be not risen, your faith is vain."

Prayer

Risen and triumphant Savior, I follow in your train with all who call you God and Lord. Amen.

Try This

If Christ didn't rise from the dead, what does your faith mean to you? If Christ didn't rise, what does that say about your sins? If Christ didn't rise, where are your loved ones, now fallen asleep? (Name them, those whom you have buried, and boldly say it, "lost.") "But now is Christ risen from the dead."

Christ Makes a Difference

The reason the world does not know us is that it did not know [Jesus]. 1 John 3:1

Isn't there some tragedy in the fact that the line between Christians and non-Christians seems to be getting blurry of late? We could celebrate that fact, if we could convince ourselves that the leveling has been upward, that the world was moving toward the great and Triune God. Alas, the movement has been downward, and no one can deny it. Christians are becoming so much like the people of this world, and the world is becoming so totally entrenched in the hearts of Christians, that you can't tell the difference without a great deal of minute investigation. We are supposed to be "a chosen people," we who profess to be Christian, set apart from the rest of the merchandise. We are supposed to have a unique word to drop into everybody's ear. We are meant to speak for God in a darkened world. Yet our lives, the style of them, and our words, the sound of them, don't confess a very noticeable contrast to the world we inhabit.

God has set us here to make a difference. That means our proclamation to our neighbors can't just mumble in its beard, and the bulletin boards which are our lives must display announcements with more than entertainment value. When we blow the bugle, it must sound as if we believe the good news that we herald. We need to speak up, not on every subject under the sun, but for the difference Christ makes. (Too often we talk as if we've been given the inside scoop on things we know nothing about.) We need to speak out loud and clear for what "we do know" and what "we have seen," namely that God has freely given his Son to die that we may live. And we must say that, not in a soft-toned, apologetic way, but with a vigor that leaves no doubt whose we are and where we fit, or don't, in this world.

Prayer

Remind me daily, dear Lord, that I am in the world but not of it. Help me become less like the people of this world and more like a citizen of heaven's fair home. Amen.

Try This

Identify three specifics in which God's child and the world should differ. Live the difference.

❖

Ultimate Meaning

I am . . . the truth. John 14:6

When Jesus rose on Easter morning it meant that everything that he had ever said was true. Easter verifies all of Christ's claims. Easter means that Jesus was not a strange character on a wild ego trip, that he was not being outrageous when he claimed what no person has ever claimed, what no person can ever claim—"I am . . . the truth."

Truth has lost status in our day. We are not as eager as people used to be to root around until we finally uncover ultimate meaning. There was a time when some looked for truth for the same reason others climbed a mountain, because it was there. Not any more. We'd rather monkey around with an intelligent guess to see where it will lead us, or test some hypothesis to find out if it works. We have developed an easy going tolerance for inaccuracy, as long as it doesn't hurt us too badly, and the phrase "margin of error" is descriptive of a way of life. But Easter maintains that somewhere behind our search for the useful and our struggle for survival, there is a key, something in whose light what everything else is all about becomes clear— truth.

"I am the truth." I wonder if we realize how startling a claim that is. It means that when scientists have boiled all the fluid out of their test tubes, they will find Jesus, and when astronauts have swarmed up and down the slopes of all the known planets, they will find Jesus. It means behind all the seeming senselessness called birth and life and highway driving and death, the meaning, the only meaning, it has is Jesus. His way is the way. His life is the life. His truth is the truth. He is the truth.

Prayer

I seek no farther, eternal Son of God, for you are your Father's revealing of all that life means. In you I find purpose and significance for this time and for eternity. And in you I find my hope. Amen.

Try This

Finish these sentences: In Jesus I discover that I am in this world to . . . Because of Jesus I look at my death and see that it is . . .

Practice What You Preach

We pray this in order that you may live a life worthy
of the Lord and may please him in every way:
bearing fruit in every good work. Colossians 1:10

The people who are representative of this world like to tell Christians to "practice what you preach." There's not much use or accuracy denying the charge that most of us still flounder a long way from the finishing line when it comes to Christ-like living. What makes that doubly devastating is that it dulls our witness to those outside the Christian pale, and affords them a nifty handle for swinging the cudgel of disinterest at the Gospel of Christ.

The church, like everyone else, is subject to faddism. That is, every year or two we all go chasing down the road after the newest emphasis. Church growth is near the top of the heap at the moment. Several years back it was evangelism. And when it was, there was a lot of talk about pre-evangelism. Pre-evangelism is what qualifies the validity of our witness by what our daily lives exclaim. It isn't that hard really to say "God is love." "Jesus saves" can even be touted by way of a bumpersticker. You might find it quite easy to tell neighbors and folks on the assembly line with you that God makes a caring, loving community out of people which we call church. But the words, if we as individuals, or you and your fellow Christians as a congregation, or all of us together as the Christian enterprise on earth, fall short of our claim to be loving and caring, and come off as "sounding brass and tinkling cymbal." Our actions cast a shadow of doubt over the inquiring heart, and our words of witness, "God is love" and "Jesus saves," become suspect in the hearer's mind.

Pre-evangelism means creating a receptive atmosphere—through a kind, courageous, gentle, loving, honest life—for the words of witness we want to share. Our witness is not only what we say, but what we are—what we have been made, through Christ.

Prayer

Let nothing in my life and conduct belie the wonder of your grace and love. Instead, lead people to see in me what wondrous things your power and tenderness can do. Amen.

Try This

Isolate five things which are distinctly Christian. Galatians 5:22–23 will help. Determine specifically five things that you can do today to demonstrate these Christian virtues.

Fruit of the Spirit

Blessed are the meek, for they will inherit the earth.
Matthew 5:5

Have you ever noticed how frequently the concept of "meekness" insinuates itself into the pages of the Bible? Numbers 12:3 (KJV) tells us that Moses was "very meek," if you can believe that. You get the idea that Jeremiah wasn't being particularly pushy when he was dealing with "all the officials" (Jer. 26:12–14). Simon Peter, years later, recalled the meekness of Christ and could hardly believe it (1 Pet. 2:23). Even St. Paul, instructing Timothy in the skills of ministry, calls for it (2 Tim. 2:25, KJV).

Meekness is always a positive thing when you come across it in the Bible, a desirable trait. And have you noticed how little of it there is, even in the church, or how meanly it is regarded by most? We're more apt to applaud boldness. We excuse the overbearing and self-important in admiration of the way in which they seem to get things done.

The dictionary says meekness is patience and mildness, disinclination to anger or resentment, gentleness, kindness. You won't find many words like that, or related notions, in catalogs of characteristics of effective management or "ways to the top." But you do find them in biblical catalogs of Christian attitudes and spiritual "fruits" (Gal. 5:22–23).

Meekness! Funny, isn't it? We'd probably get a lot farther down the road with our assignments on the job, our efforts in the church, or our goals in life, accomplish a great deal more of what we have been commissioned to do, if we practiced a little bit more of it. People may not always regard meekness highly or covet it much. But the Bible does. In the Bible it is an honored "fruit of the spirit."

Prayer

In your eyes, dear Lord, it is the meek who are blessed. How different the mind of this world. Let me reflect your mind and thus bring a touch of that which can make life in this world a little more like heaven. Amen.

Try This

On the first occasion which presents itself, opt against boldness and brashness and choose meekness, preferring others. It may leave you in second place, but note how much the atmosphere improves.

The Advocate

There is . . . one mediator between God and men, the man Christ Jesus. 1 Timothy 2:5

In Proverbs 22:22–23 we are advised not to take advantage of people who stand helpless in the courtroom because God will argue their case for them. We've got an arrangement like that in our nation's legal system. If a person stands alone and helpless to see to his own defense in our courts, the government provides for him, gets a public defender to argue his case for him.

Well, that's just too apt a parable and picture of our human situation to let it go limping off into the dark without at least a passing wave at it. Who's going to argue about the helpless state of affairs in which we find ourselves today? At every level of life—world, nation, church, and, worst of all, at that level where our individual hearts lie open and bared and our private lives are up for judgment—we are beyond ourselves, over our heads in deep water, unable to throw together any kind of adequate defense. We've nobody to argue our case for us, and not much of a case to argue under any circumstances. Surely that sums up our private situation. Not only are we helpless, we are so vulnerable. Anybody can take advantage and pick on us, and many do.

But there is one to argue our case for us, the great advocate. He is the champion sent by God to stand up for us, Jesus Christ. We needn't feel so helpless. Those who seek to take advantage of our vulnerability better watch their step. Whatever impasse you have reached in your personal relationships and your daily walk through life, a way is being found out of your woods, and the divine public defender is ready to plead your case. And, best of all, he will argue your case on the basis of his perfection, not yours. From helpless and vulnerable to confident and strong, just like that!

Prayer

My prayer is simply praise that you, dear Lord and holy defender, speak up on my behalf before the eternal judgment seat and, arguing on the basis of your innocence, convince the great judge of my own. Amen.

Try This

The next time you feel helpless and without defense, go off alone to remind yourself that there is one who loves you and speaks for you and establishes your goodness and rightness and worth.

Look to the Cross

*May I never boast except in the cross of our Lord
Jesus Christ, through which the world has been
crucified to me, and I to the world.* Galatians 6:14

The cross of Jesus is the only real hope we have, and we ought to stop looking for anything else to help us. Isaac Watts got the idea: "Our God, our help in ages past, our hope for years to come." All time, the past, the present, and the future, sways gently, held up always by the ageless cross. The cross isn't something past and done; it is something going on right now. You can grab hold of it, too, like Luther did, or Augustine, or the apostle Paul. It can lift you, too, and carry you along. There is no reason why you can't take the load off your shoulders and hand it over to Christ, because the cross is holding up the world today. Now, right now, God through Jesus is forgiving sins and protecting the frightened and carrying the lame, the halt, and the blind, and breaking that dreadful drift of evil which is the devil, himself, and this world, and our flesh.

But the cross isn't only our hope. It's our strategy. As you look at it, it dawns on you that here is a better way of treating each other than we have ever thought of before. Looking at that cross, you begin to realize that it's not just putting up with the evil that's done to us and forgiving it, or turning the other cheek; it's answering evil with good and with love, the way Jesus did. We are forever telling ourselves that some emergency exists so we can't do it Jesus' way just now. We keep putting it off. Yet, there is absolutely nothing that stops us from doing it Jesus' way right now.

God's purpose for this world can be fulfilled. At least we can come a whole lot closer to it if we give his strategy, his way, a try. Look at the cross. We can quit expecting anything to come out of anything else.

Prayer
This, on the cross, dear Savior, is your gift to me by which I am forgiven, empowered, and renewed. This, on the cross, is your risk in me for the future of your kingdom. Keep your cross before my eyes and through it make me victor. Amen.

Try This
In this day's doings, in each case when you deal with anyone, ask first how Christ has dealt with you. Then follow in his way.

The Difference That Christ Makes

When they hurled their insults at him, he did not retaliate; when he suffered, he made no threats.
1 Peter 2:23

Think of the adjustments Simon Peter had to make in order to feel comfortable in the kingdom of God. We all have to make adjustments, of course. But old Peter had a long way to come from where his instincts had him when Jesus appeared on his horizon, and there is something uniquely warm and winsome and remarkable about this crusader, sitting there in his old age, shaking his head, still hardly able to believe what he himself had heard Jesus say. He recorded it in his letter, "When they hurled insults at him, he did not retaliate; when he suffered, he made no threats."

What Jesus didn't do struck the old fisherman as being, at the very least, totally unique. Jesus showed no resentment, no bitterness. He didn't lash out or strike back when he was manhandled and hurt. Jesus was different all right. And he insisted that those who wanted to be counted among his followers be different too. "What are you doing" Jesus wanted to know, "more than others?" (Matt. 5:47). The average wasn't good enough. Christianity can't live without the comment that it stirs. To stir comment it needs to be different, and better, than everything else. As long as we respond to life's disappointments and inequities like everyone else, there's nothing to commend us or what we have over anything else in this world.

But what a difference! Peter couldn't believe it. And I'm not sure we always like it. Jesus' followers are thoughtful where everyone else has ceased to care. They forgive when it's not only foolish, but dangerous to do so. They are generous where someone is bound to take advantage of their generosity. That's different. People may look at us out of the corners of their eyes, but they won't be bored. They will be interested, interested in the difference that Christ makes.

Prayer

Make me to shine like a light in the dark, O Christ, that men may see my uniqueness and come to glorify the Father through whose grace I have been remade to be different. Amen.

Try This

Ask, "How am I different from my neighbors?" Find five specific differences which mark you as Christian. Ask the Holy Spirit's help as you arrange for them to appear from now on in your life.

The Will of God

The world and its desires pass away, but the man who does the will of God lives forever. 1 John 2:17

This old world which we call home is doomed. Everything in it, the things which you can see and touch and smell, is listed in God's calendar on his dated day of devastation. The Bible leaves no doubt about it. The world passes away. You don't have to be a Bible student, of course, to know that things in general are running down. Some purely scientific types are pondering the possibilities of an early end. Someone has noticed that we have used up 90 percent of our mercury, 85 percent of our silver, and 60 percent of our copper and oil. The bottom of the ocean affords some hope, of course. The point is, God doesn't, not that kind of hope.

An hour is coming. That will be the day. In that day and in that hour all the great achievements of history will crumble, and the cities and highways and bridges and dams will come tumbling down. Your house, your bank account, and your business, all have been marked by the finger of God. The masses of mankind act as if we are going to live forever. When you think you are going to live forever, you go about trying to suck the last drop of pleasure out of life. That's why St. John says, "The world and its desires pass away." That's a whole lot of passing away.

"But the man who does the will of God lives forever."

What is that will? God's will is our salvation. He "wants all men to be saved" (1 Tim. 2:4). To bring us to salvation he had the Bible written. To bring us to salvation he had the church established. To bring us to salvation he sent his Son into the world to suffer in our stead and perish in our place. To bring us to salvation is his will. "Do this and you will live" (Luke 10:28). But what is left to do? All of it is done, has been done, for us in Jesus. To believe that is to do God's will and thereby "live forever."

Prayer

High and lifted up, nailed to that monstrous throne, you are God's will for me. Your life and death, O Jesus, and your resurrection are my everlasting hope and glory. Amen.

Try This

List the five possessions from which you derive most pleasure. These are destined for destruction. But you shall live forever if you trust Christ and thus fulfill the will of God.

Thank God

Do not be anxious about anything, but in every-thing, by prayer and petition, with thanksgiving, present your requests to God. Philippians 4:6

If there is one thing we don't seem to have much control over, it's this set of nerves which keeps assailing us on every side morning, noon, and night, and at the most unwelcome moments in between. Health, finances, what other people think of us, getting caught, where does one end the list of things in day-to-day life which keep us on the raw edge of anxiety?

But St. Paul doesn't leave us thinking how, if he has nothing better to say, it would be better if he said nothing at all. No. He tells you the secret for overcoming anxiety. "In everything, by prayer and petition, present your requests to God." There it is, the Christian way with every trouble in the world, our secret for serenity: bring God into it. Undergird it with the love of heaven.

But it's that little phrase, "with thanksgiving," that's got my attention, and I'd like it to get hold of yours. Coming in a letter about anxiety, it's very significant. When you are in the doldrums, feeling fretful and unhappy, and people around are doing everything they can, it seems, to beat you down, then remember the other side of the ledger. The credit side has some entries, too, isn't that so? "Praise the Lord, O my soul, and forget not all his benefits" (Ps. 103:2). I should say: health, if you still have it, friends, and beauty in the world around you. Don't forget that God is still forgiving you at Jesus' cross, at the very moment when anxiety has got its stranglehold on you. The big thing, anyway, is under control. You can thank God for that.

Anxious about something? Take it to the Lord in prayer. And remember all the good things too. Take it to him "with thanksgiving."

Prayer

Father, I thank you that there are always glorious blessings from your lavish hand for which to thank you when I come to you in prayer. Temper my anxieties with the remembrance of all you do for me. Amen.

Try This

Make a list of all those things for which, even in your most anxious moments, you can thank God.

He Has His Eye on You

If I have sinned, what have I done to you, O watcher of men? Why have you made me your target? Job 7:20

Moffatt's translation is even more startling. He translates "watcher of men" with "O thou spy upon mankind." What a frightful thing to say to God, although it isn't as if the thought hasn't occurred to us before. When someone reminds you that God sees all, he is more than likely suggesting that you watch your step.

Of course, we can't just shrug off our sins. Our sins, if for no other reason, are important because of what they do to us. I'm not referring only to the glaring marks they leave on the body or the landscape, but the things which sins like selfishness, indifference, neglect, and meanness do to people. They change us, subtly, until you can hardly recognize us anymore as children of God.

Worse than that is what our sins do to God and our relationship with him. God does not spy upon our sin. Our sins do that all by themselves. "Your sin will find you out" (Num. 32:23). And punish? That's an old story and done with 2000 years ago, in Jesus, on Calvary. What looks and feels like punishment is usually nothing more than the laws of sowing and reaping. But our sins separate us from our God, insinuate this awful alienation, spoil it between us, to the point we feel as if we are God's target.

Well, in a sense we are. He had us in mind, you, when he sent his Son to die. He was aiming at our forgiveness, yours, when he let Jesus feel the full brunt of his anger up there on the cross. "God made him who had no sin to be sin for us" (2 Cor. 5:21). He targeted us with his love. Maybe

Job stumbled on it, after all. God does take dead aim at us when he sends Jesus to be a substitute, sends him to become "sin for us," so that we can become the "righteousness of God."

Prayer

Heavenly Father, I welcome your eye on me. I cherish your attention. For through Jesus all your commerce with me is for my eternal good. Amen.

Try This

Identify ten ways in which you need the watchful eye of God on you today. Imagine your life without God's attention and his care.

Out of the Heart

Since we live by the Spirit, let us keep in step with the Spirit. Galatians 5:25

There are many people who are afraid to do a little good for someone, exercise a little kindness, overlook a little weakness, risk a little involvement, or invest a little effort on someone's behalf, and all for fear that it won't pay off in the long run. There are some notable exceptions, of course, and the most obvious walk across the pages of the New Testament. Living, for a lot of the early Christians, was an exercise in investment, a matter of rolling up your sleeves and putting something into this business of life, right here, where you are and with what you've got, without a great deal of concern for what you were going to get out of it. You could speak well of people, treat them kindly and forgive them openly without measuring first if they lived up to your standards or met your expectations. It wasn't what they would do in response that concerned you.

St. Paul talked a lot about that. He was a great one for pointing out that what you do for people—what you spend on their behalf and invest in their well being—is the result of what is in your heart by reason of Jesus having set up housekeeping there, and not the result of what was in their hearts which might qualify them for your good graces. He coined a term for it, "fruit of the spirit." What it means, simply, is that what you do, also for others, you do because of the way you are, because Jesus lives in your heart, not because of the way others are.

The Spirit of God has made us alive in Christ. Now it's a matter that those of us who live in the Spirit would keep in step by the power of the Spirit.

Prayer

Spirit of God, lead me to be true to the Christ who has saved me, by fulfilling his standards, all because he dwells in me. Amen.

Try This

Pick two friends whom you admire. Do something good for them. Then pick two acquaintances whom you do not admire. Do the same for them.

In God We Trust

Our help is in the name of the Lord. Psalm 124:8

Christians are wont to hang on to God for dear life.

It's unique in this world to speak of hope, and then point outside yourself as the reason for it. The world around us is more apt to thump its chest and hook its thumbs into its armpits and find its comfort in its own considerable powers. But Christians lift their eyes to "the hills" (Ps. 121:1), God's hills. That, they figure, is where their help comes from. "Hasten," they say, "O God, to save me" (Ps. 70:1). "God is our refuge and strength" (Ps. 46:1), they readily admit.

People think the peculiarity of the "peculiar people" in 1 Peter 2:9 (KJV) derives from the things which they don't do, like laughing hard or going to the races. Some, the more astute, equate Christianity with the things that Christians do, like loving when others hate or being patient when others lose their heads. That is different, to be sure, and very Christian, indeed. But the peculiarity, the essence of what makes Christian people odd, really, lies in the fact that a Christian is one who has let go his grip on his own boot straps and, having done so, lays hold of the promises of God. Christians dare to put their trust in God rather than man—rather than in themselves.

Now and again this uniqueness, this focus upon God as our hope for years to come, blurs or even deserts us altogether. When it does, there is nothing to distinguish us from the people in the world around us. Then we, like they, begin to deal with each other on the basis of our own cunning and deception and bluff. But when we eschew that kind of misplaced self-reliance, then are we his disciples, indeed, and folks around begin to scratch their heads and mutter, "What manner of people is this?"

Prayer

You, dearest Lord Jesus, who have taught me the ways of God, make firm my trust in what he does for me through you. Help me fall back on everlasting arms. Amen.

Try This

Count the ways you rely in one day on your ability and strength. Now count the ways in which God sustains and keeps you. Where, really, is your daily help? Who fails? Who doesn't?

Free from Fear

Perfect love drives out fear. 1 John 4:18

You don't need me to tell you how appropriate any word which helps us cope with our fears is to this day and age. We live in a flood tide of overwhelming fear. There are many who will not go out after dark, or sit on their own porch steps because of this hideous development called "drive-by shootings." Shopping malls are invitations to assault and battery and worse. You don't know when the person in the car alongside you on the highway is going to grow angry and turn on you in violence.

But we're no strangers to less lurid fears which can be equally debilitating. It's these that claim our attention here. We are so afraid of the opinion people have of us, we spend much of our time trying to build ourselves up in the eyes of others. We nervously measure ourselves by other people's yardsticks. Where did we get the idea that we must be so terribly concerned with what others think of us? Not from the New Testament. There we are told that we should be concerned about what people think, not of what we are, but of what we have been given, namely forgiveness for the past and another chance for the future.

Sometimes we are afraid even of ourselves. We are afraid of what we aren't. We find it difficult to accept our limitations. Confronted by real life, running up against rebuff and failure and frustration, we find it hard to accept our limits and interpret them in terms of failure.

"Perfect love drives out fear." The perfect love of God in Jesus meets our fears head on and masters them. In fact, that love takes our minds off our failures and focuses them on that glorious "failure" up on Calvary, which succeeded at last to set us free of fear of what we are and of what others think of us.

Prayer

Give me peace of heart and mind, dear Lord, by the assurance that you love me, that you value me, that you are my protection. Amen.

Try This

Each time you wonder what someone thinks of you, ask yourself what Jesus thinks. His love gives you comfort. His judgment gives direction to your life.

Knee Bent and Body Bowed

At the name of Jesus every knee should bow.
Philippians 2:10

There can be no doubt, if you remember the garden of Gethsemane, that not only Jesus' hands and feet and side were involved in the process of redemption, but his knees too. And if there is anything our knees can do for him, you will agree, he is fully entitled to it.

Spiritual rheumatism is a widespread affliction which must not be allowed to assume epidemic proportions among us. On our knees is a fitting posture for us when we approach our God. We need not be committed to a high, liturgical approach when we come to the mercy seat of God. You can surely speak to God standing upright or lying prone or seated. But there is no posture I know more in keeping with what we need to say to him than knees bent and bodies bowed. "God, have mercy on me, a sinner" is what we need most to tell our Lord. The pharisee, the Bible says, stood up to pray. I bet he did.

Knees have a history all their own in Scripture. Adam's shook, at least I would assume they did, as he hid among the bushes in the Garden of Eden. Daniel tells us, the king's "knees knocked together" (Dan. 5:6). That isn't so surprising when you remember that at the moment, a disembodied finger was writing his doom upon the wall. Seven thousand pairs of knees refused to bow to Baal (1 Kings 19:18). Jesus knelt and "an angel from heaven appeared to him and strengthened him" (Luke 22:41–43). St. Paul's sea legs may have been so-so one morning on the Mediterranean, but his knees were steady. "Last night an angel of the God whose I am and whom I serve stood beside me and said, 'Do not be afraid, Paul' " (Acts 27:23–24).

Knees strengthened with might because they have bent down before the throne of God's grace stand steady and firm.

Prayer

Humbly I kneel; confident I rise again. You are my God, and I bow down in adoration and in praise before your throne. Bless me, Lord, this day. Amen.

Try This

Tonight, when you say your prayers, really come knee bent and body bowed, to remind yourself of the majesty of your God and the immensity of the privilege which is yours to come to him in prayer.

The Christians

As you received Christ Jesus as Lord, continue to live in him. Colossians 2:6

It was in Antioch where Christ's disciples were first called Christians. That was not, as it originated, intended to be a compliment. Nevertheless, it wouldn't have happened, would not have been needed, if those early followers of Christ hadn't been unique, hadn't made an impression because they were so different.

A good guess is that Christians were known all over town because of the things they would not do. They refused to show up at the amphitheater to watch people being slaughtered because they believed that life was the gift of God. (Of course, afterwards they stayed away, if they could, because, if they didn't, they would be the ones to be slaughtered, and all because they were so different.) And they wouldn't engage in the self-indulgence and immorality for which Antioch was so well known, because they believed their bodies were the temples of God. You wouldn't see them at the theater because of the obscenity you were bound to run into there. It was, at least in part, their refusal to participate which resulted in the tag "Christian."

What they did set them apart, as well. They lived life, and they lived it more abundantly. They gathered to worship and they dispersed to share the gospel. They prayed as if they really thought it would work. They loved one another and were outgoing and helpful to others. They became known for their patience, and they talked about hope. They had that smile which made them look like they knew something no one else knew. They were different, all right. So they got tagged with the most beautiful name of all: Christian.

Well, it didn't just come to them. They got it the hard way. They earned it by living out Jesus' love. If we're going to wear the name, too, we ought to wear it with just as much reason.

Prayer

Let people see in my life the difference you make, my Lord, and know that I am yours. Amen.

Try This

Review the week just past. Name 5 things which you did not do and 5 things you did that would help people identify you as a child of God and brother of Christ.

He Did—He Does—He Will

To him who loves us and has freed us from our sins . . .—to him be glory. Revelation 1:5

Now and again more recent translations of the Bible make a significant improvement on the familiar words coming out of the court of old King James. This is one of them. The King James version says, "Unto him that loved us . . . " But to be absolutely accurate and to come a whole lot closer to capturing the truth of the matter, the past tense should be present. That's right. Not just at Bethlehem or along the hillsides of old Galilee or up on Calvary, but here and now, today, tomorrow, and forever, all across the globe, God loves us.

We are well acquainted with the past tenses of the Holy Scripture: "Born of the Virgin Mary, suffered under Pontius Pilate, crucified, dead, buried, the third day risen from the dead." Are we as well acquainted with our religion's present tenses? The Christ who is out on our streets seeking and finding people today, the Christ who is drying the tears of the broken-hearted and soothing the pillows of the suffering and comforting the ones who go about under a deep depression from a bad, but accurate, self-image, and doing all that at this moment, how well do we know him? "To him who loves us," present tense, "be glory."

"And has freed us from our sins." There is a kind of love which never sees action, sits endlessly on the bench, and doesn't get into the game. But God's love acts, is equated with action, can't be contemplated apart from what it does about it. He loves us and has freed us. This time it's in the past tense. It's all over and done with, nothing more to do, behind us forever. You don't need to fuss or worry. You have been set free.

Spurgeon quotes an old woman: "If Jesus does save me, he shall never hear the end of it." He did save us. "To him be glory."

Prayer

Who can forgive sins but you only, O God, who for my sins are justly displeased. Yet you have sent your Son and he has died to forgive me and in him you love me every day and forever. Amen.

Try This

Review the week just past to spot two times when God exercised his love for you—alerting you to dangers, assisting you in endeavors, which by yourself would have been beyond your coping. Remember, to him who does that daily "be glory."

Not Why but How

We share in his sufferings in order that we may also share in his glory. Romans 8:17

The problems and the troubles and the terrors of life are real, and there is no handy answer a person can give to the questions which they raise. When someone wants to know what sense it all makes with a husband lying there dead, or a son who might be better off so, or a body which just lives on and on so it can soak up more pain—there's no light and merry answer at a time like that.

I'd like to start with this: this life is not the end of us. We're being gotten ready. We're here to grow into something. Whatever else God is interested in, he is interested in what you turn out to be. Not how long you live or how comfortable your life, but what you are becoming in the process—he's interested in that.

If that's true, it's almost inevitable that some sort of struggle will be involved. You can't develop any honesty unless you are tempted to lie. You can't be brave if you aren't threatened. You can't win if it isn't possible to lose.

This may not seem to be the best of all possible worlds from your point of view, but it does seem to fit God's intentions pretty well.

And the only comfort God gives us in the face of it, he gives us in Jesus. Jesus knows. He's been there. Kind, gentle as he was, he was crucified. Good friend to all, he was betrayed. Jesus knows. He doesn't promise to make it any easier. He does promise to make it possible. The night after he told his disciples how tough it was going to be, he went to Calvary to arrange for the things they would need to face it all. He bought their forgiveness with his blood; he arranged for their faith; he put in their supply of courage. He won for them their comfort. And ours. Then he sends us into a hard world.

Prayer

I ask only, Lord of my life, that you walk with me that, my hand in yours, I may walk worthy of my God. Amen.

Try This

What three things trouble you most today? What would Christ have you do in the face of them? Do them and develop into the kind of Christian God wants you to be. He is there to help.

The Peace of God

Peace I leave with you; my peace I give you. I do not give to you as the world gives. John 14:27

There's a big difference between peace of mind and the peace of God. Thousands are looking for, and some are finding, peace of mind at their psychiatrist's office. Among those who have it are the people next door who are moderately successful, fairly respectable, and who really mean it when they attribute a spectacular shot on the golf course to living right. Peace of mind is a good name for it. After all, it is peace created in and sustained by the mind. It is a degree of contentment which settles down upon the consciousness of one who has calculated his chances against the hostilities of life and concluded that, with his share of breaks, he can come through without getting too seriously hurt.

Now listen to Jesus: "Peace I leave with you; my peace I give you." Notice the difference. The peace of God is a gift, not an achievement. Peace of mind is something you can find, must find, if you're to have it. But you can't find the peace of God. It finds you. And the cross is its eyes, its hands, and its feet. It passes all understanding, because it is the forgiveness of sins. Peace of mind—peace because you've got your own ability firmly in mind—dares not talk about sins. It goes to pieces on the fact of them. God's peace is not only the opposite of peace of mind. It is the end of it. It's the abandoning of any satisfaction with the way you are managing and of contentment with your moderate success. It's letting go your grip to settle into the arms of God. Peace of mind disappears at the place where the peace of God steps in.

Now may "the peace of God which transcends all understanding guard your hearts and minds in Christ Jesus."

Prayer

Lord of my heart, guard me against all danger, particularly that which would destroy my soul. Garrison my heart and life with your angels and grant me peace. Amen.

Try This

Analyze the moments in the week just passed when you reached a comfort level with reference to anything pending. Was it your ability to cope which set you at your ease? That's peace of mind. What comforts you as far as your eternal future is concerned? Is it God's love which gives you comfort? That is the peace of God.

How to Cure a Case of Nerves

My Presence will go with you, and I will give you rest. Exodus 33:14

Have you ever taken a hard look at your restless moods? Are circumstances to blame? Can you really say, "It's not my fault"? Why do you grow irritable, or your nerves get on edge, so that you say things for which you are sorry the moment after you have said them? Why do you find it so hard to relax? Why are there days when nothing seems to go right? Why can't you sleep at night? Are you going to blame everybody else for that? I think the trouble, at least a large share of it, is in ourselves.

Think what Jesus had to put up with during his lifetime: interruptions, continual intrusion on his privacy, inconsiderate people breaking in on his day off; the nagging of those who thought they knew better how he ought to handle things; criticism, pettiness. Yet Jesus had a serene, untroubled heart.

Would you like that? Well, Jesus, of course, had all it takes to make a go of it. He knew he was up to what faced him. What about you? You "can do everything through him who gives [you] strength" (Phil. 4:13). That's the sentence of a person who won't get shook the first time life challenges. Besides, Jesus was so dedicated to the cause which prompted him to come into this world in the first place that he didn't have any trouble knowing what was important and where his priorities were. What about you? God has given you your goals and purpose. "What does the Lord require of you? To act justly and to love mercy and to walk humbly with him" (Micah 6:8). Remember what you're here for.

Next, Jesus had a pure heart. That helps bring on a good night's sleep. You too. It is possible for you to be among those who have "washed their robes and made them white in the blood of the Lamb" (Rev. 7:14). So rest easy. And finally, Jesus was in perfect fellowship with God. The last time that had happened people called it paradise. You too. That's what Calvary did, brought you back into perfect fellowship with God.

That ought to take care of the restless moods.

Prayer

I thank you, O my God, for taking away all my edgy moments and my reasons for them. Amen.

Try This

Ask why your nerves are on edge. Measure your resources, think of your purpose, bask in his forgiveness, and walk with him.

Everybody Counts

Has not God chosen those who are poor in the eyes of the world to be rich in faith? James 2:5

Do you remember Emily Dickinson's little quip: "I'm nobody. Who are you? Are you nobody too? Then there's a pair of us"? But there's another side to that coin. Where two or three are gathered together in the name of Jesus Christ, you have a crowd worth reckoning with.

Here is some good news for all those of us who are inclined to think we don't amount to much in this world. God thinks you are somebody, wants to make you somebody in the only society worth joining, the body of Christ. If you want to see who they are whom God thinks are real somebodies, whom he thought it was worth going to Calvary for, dying for, stand under the cross. Look around. Sinners, pretty commonplace sinners, at that. Just like us.

Your part and mine in this life may seem trivial and of little consequence, but our faithfulness to the way we carry out our part is not trivial. Not in the least. Why is it we think only the solo parts count in the orchestra of Jesus Christ? The truth is there are no solo parts in the music which accompanies the march of the church militant through human history. Only ordinary parts are to be found there, a little toot on the piccolo over here, a tap on the drum over there, the quiet hum of a viola. But put them all together and let Jesus wield the baton, why, it becomes a sym-phony, the powerful march of the children of God through the history of this world.

So don't talk "nobodies," not after what Jesus has

done to sanctify each of us and the part we play in the story of his church on earth. What you and I do for Christ, with him going on before, matters. It's really all that matters.

Prayer

Teach me, Savior in heaven, the true value of each little thing I do. Keep me mindful that it all fits into the mosaic of God's purpose and his plan. Amen.

Try This

Subtract from the events of one day what would not happen in our country if each Christian in it decided, for that day, not to do any Christian act at all. Visualize what would happen if every Christian in our nation lived up to his or her full potential as a child of God. Even just one day.

All One in Christ

But if we walk in the light, as he is in the light, we have fellowship with one another. 1 John 1:7

There is a whole new theory which has stirred a lot of interest and engendered a lot of support, which claims that churches—congregations—in order to be "success-ful," that is grow large, must be more or less homogeneous, made up of related kinds and sorts. Birds of a feather, the cliche insists, flock together.

What is a great deal more startling, and bespeaks the genius of the Christian church, (more accurately the genius of its heart and soul, Christ Jesus) is its ability to homogenize into compatible and considerate and loving groups people of totally opposite backgrounds and cultures and ideas. It started back there in the salad days of Christianity. It was Christianity, after all, which took a man who had been a haughty, practicing Pharisee, an elite Hebrew who made sure everybody knew it, Saul of Tarsus was his name, and suddenly had him baring his heart to slaves and barbarians, calling them, "my brothers in the faith." Ladies from the Roman court, with regal blood flowing through their veins, took the cup and shared it with some homeless wanderer from the streets. You get a glimpse of it, sometimes, at altars in the church today—teenage boys with funny haircuts kneeling alongside their "oh so proper" elders, Southeast Asians sharing the cup of blessing with immigrants from Lithuania, African Americans, German tradesmen, flighty chatterboxes, and Ph.D.s.

And when you put us all together, we spell Christian church. Of course, we have a commonality, one thing which binds us into a fellowship and overcomes, or overlooks, at least, so many more things that make us different. That commonality is Christ. We all, each of us, can say, "I believe in Jesus Christ," and we can say it together.

Prayer

You have made me, dear Father, one with all who profess the Christ. Let me glory in that love of Christ which triumphs over all the forces which would pull us apart and makes us, together, the children of God. Amen.

Try This

Name three fellow Christians who are diametrically different from you in temperament, or interests, or background. Celebrate your oneness.

God Always Wins

Our light and momentary troubles are achieving for us an eternal glory. 2 Corinthians 4:17

I don't care what you call it, "ups and downs," "just one of those days," or "my share," we are all acquainted on a first name basis with that rhythm of life which every now and again brings us face to face with the trouble we get into just by being alive and taking up our share of the space required to house the human race.

And we've got this overwhelming urge to explain it. Some of us claim that a gall bladder attack, or a cut in pay is just God's way of getting even with us for all those times when we have tromped, willy-nilly, on his will and wishes. What that idea calls for is the quick reminder that God punished Jesus for all our sins, and that to insist he punishes us is to reject, and thereby nullify, that monumental sacrifice called Calvary, a rejection God does punish.

Others claim there is no such thing as trouble, really. It's all in our heads. They've built some rival religions around that notion, but they aren't doing too well. Most of us have too much firsthand experience with trouble to seriously believe there isn't any. The Bible explanation makes more sense. There is such a thing as trouble and Satan pulls its strings. "This is your hour," Jesus said, as much to Satan as to anyone, "—when darkness reigns" (Luke 22:53).

But the Bible says more. The Bible says that it is often precisely in the moment when Satan is exercising his "power of the dark" that God has his most bright and shining hour. That was certainly true at Calvary. At the very moment when Satan was having his most powerful impact on the world, God was culminating his most ambitious plan to save us. In fact, God took Satan's finest hour and used it to crush Satan forever. Calvary, in the long run, belongs to God. That ought have something to say to you about your hour of darkness.

Prayer

Hold me and heal me, blessed Jesus, through the hardest hours so that I may praise you in the hours of my victory. Amen.

Try This

Look back upon the hardest moments in your life. See God at work in them. Identify the good things in your life, the strengths, the blessings, which he has brought to you through those dark moments.

"When Chill Dew Glistens on the Brow"

During those days men will seek death. Revelation 9:6

Most of us would be surprised to discover how many there are who have seriously entertained the notion that death might very well offer the solution to their problems. There are Christian agencies with night and day phone service given over to convincing someone under desperate conditions that a voluntary walk through the doorway marked "life exit—one way" is not a solution at all, even if it is the only doorway at hand. It's a false dawn, the idea of death bringing to rest the troubles that burden us. The last estate of the person who chooses that way is worse than the first. Having said that much, and presuming that most of you accept it, what are we left with? Just this, unless someone can show us different, death, rather than spelling the end of all our troubles, can be the worst one we have got.

Everything from vitamin pills to safety zones are signs of our preoccupation with the dread of dying. Most of us don't like to contemplate the day when "someone else will dress [us] and lead [us] where [we] do not want to go" (John 21:18). What disturbs us is that picture we have of God totaling up the pluses and minuses of life and determining our everlasting future on the basis of what we have done or haven't, and what we have been or failed to be. I'd venture to guess that a lot of the good that's done these days is manacled by the suspicion that when we die we are going to need some kind of favorable record to refer to before a faceless, awful judge who keeps watching every move we make.

But just because it is that way doesn't mean it has to be. When our last hour comes and the door of death opens, there is one on the other side waiting, one who died to be there when we come, who will take us by the hand and say, "I've been here before. I know the way. I've made arrangements for your arrival. There'll be no reckoning in your case. I've taken care of that for you. Welcome home." His name is Jesus.

Prayer

Come, O Lord Jesus. Set us free from death and every evil. Amen.

Try This

Read Psalm 23:4 and Proverbs 14:32, replacing the

pronouns with your name and equating "the righteous" with yourself.

Dedicated to High Purpose

So whether you eat or drink or whatever you do, do all for the glory of God. 1 Corinthians 10:31

An editorial writer was waxing eloquent, and not a little hot under the collar, about the conversion of Canadian pines into paper which was, in turn, used almost exclusively to carry the "inanities" of "printed trash." Canadian pines, he pointed out, and I have every reason to believe he had some special insights backing him up, or maybe he just thrilled to look at them, are outstanding examples of God's creative hand at its best. "Trash," he added cryptically, "is trash."

It sets one's mind going. God has created so many things for high purpose. Not the least of his creatures is mankind—our minds, our voices, our capacity to lose ourselves in contemplation of and appreciation for the beautiful things you find in the world. So frequently we employ these exquisite gems of God's creating for such mundane purposes: making a dollar, filling out income tax returns, producing "how to" books on window installation. Worse, much worse, we contribute these considerable gifts to the activities of blasphemy, pornography, hatred, and strife.

It's a matter of goals. Once you have given yourself over to the immorality of minimum goals and inferior values, God's gifts are wasted, and the high purposes and lofty accomplishments they are capable of are lost and gone forever. Someone once said, "If I were an American I would judge everything in it alongside the Grand Canyon. I would ask if it is worthy of a country which has in it the Grand Canyon of the Colorado."

Might we not well measure ourselves and our accomplishments, asking if they are worthy of a life which has Jesus Christ in it?

Prayer

Help me, precious Savior, never to be satisfied with less than my best. You were not satisfied to give me anything less than yours. Amen.

Try This

Find five activities from your day which required some skill, some ability. Are each of these the best that you could do, the loftiest use you could make of your talent?

A Happy Ending

He is not here; he has risen. Matthew 28:6

Good Friday has its Easter. "The third day he rose again from the dead." The cross was not the end of everything; it wasn't an end at all. A woman playwright complained to William Dean Howells about what she called "the American addiction to the happy ending." "They insist always on the good guys living happily ever after." Mr. Howells agreed. "What the American public wants is a tragedy which ends happily." Not just Americans, I would wager. Everybody.

Well, for that you can't do better than the Good Friday-Easter episode. "He breathed his last," Luke describes Jesus' death (Luke 23:46). It was tragic. Here was the God of all good, the King of kindness and love, martyred at the hands of utterly wicked people. But there is more to the story. The tragedy concludes with a happy ending after all. "On the first day of the week" (Luke 24:1), he rose from the dead.

Indeed, the Christian story is the story of tragedy with a happy ending, not only, but particularly, the story of Christ. Your story too. Your stories, one after the other. There was a time when you were the epitome of tragedy, of everything that can go wrong. "You were dead in your transgressions and sins" (Eph. 2:1). But that wasn't, isn't, the end of the story. God in Christ has laid hold of you, forgiven you, renewed you, and now he even uses you to do his will on earth as it is done in heaven. And what Jesus has done for your soul he does with all the deeds of your hands, where your feet take you, what your lips say. Jesus redeems all of life from destruction. It all has been given a happy ending, and in Jesus we live happily ever after.

Prayer

God of life and death and life again, everlasting, I praise you for making my last estate a happy one, and that what was destined to be my personal tragedy has been reversed by your sacrifice and resurrection to have the happiest ending of all, life eternal. Amen.

Try This

Ask yourself what would be your disposition if today was the end, the absolute end, of everything. You don't want to think about it? St. Paul thinks you should. Read 1 Corinthians 15:17.

❖

Trust and Obey

To obey is better than sacrifice. 1 Samuel 15:22

George Washington, on one occasion, complained that his plans were being held up because his subordinates wouldn't do what he asked until he had explained the rationale behind his commands. He hoped, he said, the day would come when they had enough confidence in him to obey without question. Parents know that kind of frustration. So do some bosses. Jesus, I'd wager, knows it too.

We are in the habit of shoring up the rubrics of Christianity with explanations which detail why those rubrics are good for us. Honesty is, we explain, the best policy. Not that it ought to matter. If our Lord tells us to be honest, that ought to settle it. Putting the best construction on everything puts you in a position where you are right more often than not. That, I have found, is true, but that is not the point.

Putting the best construction on everything is God's way for his people. (See the Eighth Commandment.) "Turn the other cheek," "walk the second mile," "do good to all men." There is little doubt that this would be an immeasurably improved world to live in if we did what these commands of God request. But the motive needs to be our trust in Christ and our desire to do his will. And if turning the other cheek now and again wins you a black eye or a pain in the neck, so be it. God's will be done. George Washington saw the problem as a matter of trust, wanting his subordinates to think of him as trustworthy. Jesus tops the list when it comes to "trustworthy." So, instead of holding out your hand for an explanation when the way of God is set before you, try the gallantry and experience the thrill of doing what God wants, no questions asked.

Prayer

Your will, my God, be done, by me, because it is your will. Your judgments are past finding out and your logic doesn't always make my kind of sense. I obey because you are my Lord and king. Amen.

Try This

Read Exodus 20:7, 8, 12, 16. Determine one way you can obey each command. Do it without question, even if it promises to be unproductive or counterproductive. Later assess the upshot. Is it worth trusting God implicitly?

Boring by Conviction

I resolved to know nothing while I was with you
except Jesus Christ and him crucified. 1 Corinthians 2:2

John Milton complained about the burden of having to "blow a harsh blast on the trumpet" when it would be so much more pleasant to say gentle things. Mothers and fathers must stop at times to contemplate the glory of the day when they can exchange the words, "No, no," for something purely positive and totally constructive.

It takes a special kind of courage to haul out the same old warnings, the over-used sentences, to alert the world around us to the dangers it is courting with its self-seeking and its cruelty and its inhumanity to men. The curse of history is how we are destined to make its mistakes all over, again and again. And in there, somewhere, there are voices repeating the same calls to "watch it," with little more success than they managed the first time they were spoken.

When the world around us ignores for the seventh time, or the seventieth, the call of the Christian prophet to repent and look to the Lord Jesus for life and safety and a future, it takes a special kind of resolve and intrepidness to confront that world with the same, old story. We might wish at times that we had something new to offer a world that wasn't too excited about what we had to say in the first place. Is it boring, our message of God's grace?

Granted that we need to express that precious Gospel in the most winsome and inviting terms we can muster. But our answer to people's problems doesn't change just because they didn't care much for the words the first time they heard them. If humanity is going to be boring enough to pose the same, old problem, we will be boring enough to repeat the same, old answer—Jesus and his cross. Only we are boring by conviction.

Prayer

Do not permit me, Lord of my life, ever to draw back from my commitment to the Gospel of Christ Jesus. Let me repeat again and again that blessed story. If it needs revitalizing for people at last to listen, let that come from my conviction and enthusiasm. Whatever the challenge humanity poses, let Jesus always be my answer.

Try This

Plot out three ways to say that Jesus, God's Son, so loved this world and everyone in it, that he lived and died for us that we might live forever. Then find someone to express that to, using all three ways.

Body Parts

The body is a unit, though it is made up of many parts; . . . So it is with Christ. 1 Corinthians 12:12

St. Paul makes a point quite worth repeating in the twelfth chapter of his first letter to the Christians in Corinth. It is eminently worth your while to read that excellent chapter. It's all based on the presumption that we who are Christians together make up the body of Christ.

Around the fifteenth verse Paul makes the point. One remarkable thing, worth contemplating, is how very well the individual members of your body relate to one another. You never hear your right arm running down your left, or even acting as if it would like to now and again. And this in spite of the fact that old lefty doesn't really pull its share of the load, and couldn't, weak as it is. Your right arm doesn't get all upset that, when the work is done, the left arm gets as much credit for it as the right. Being stronger it just naturally takes over the bulk of the work, carries some of the burdens which might naturally fall to its counterpart over on the other side. And if your left arm ever gets in trouble or is hurt, the right arm asks no questions, doesn't raise its eyebrows in obvious impatience and disgust, but instantly, without thinking it through, pushes right on over and holds the wound or rubs the bruise.

That's such an apt description of the way it ought to work with Christians. St. Paul can't help but use it, calling us all together Christ's body and thinking of us separately as its members. It keeps cropping up, this picture for the holy Christian church, all through the great Apostle's letters. You can see a hundred ramifications in that picture. And you can put them to work in a hundred different ways.

Prayer
Make me a contributing, helping, loving member of your body, holy Savior, so that, with my fellow Christians, together we may do your will and make your kingdom come. Amen.

Try This
Review the week just past. List the things you did in it which belie your one-body membership with other Christians. Think of one fellow member of Christ's body. What you will you do next week in relationship to him or her?

Not Busy?

We hear that some among you are idle. They are not busy. 2 Thessalonians 3:11

What would be your response if you received a visit, along about the middle of November, from a uniformed officer, and he said to you, "Get your jacket. Come along. You are under arrest. You did not vote early this month and now you must defend yourself against the charge that you have contributed to the destruction of democracy"? Imagine that someone, perfectly capable of making a gift to the Red Cross or the drive to eradicate muscular dystrophy, has joined the majority and done nothing about it. Now he is approached with the question, "What have you got against those little children starving in Africa? What has prejudiced you against people who are diseased?" Or get this one: On Sunday a church officer comes to the house and finds you in the middle of the *Sunday Times* in bathrobe and slippers. What he says is, "Why have you chosen to destroy the holy Christian church?"

The charges, of course, are unfounded. At best they are the result of an enormous exaggeration. Yet, they have a point to make. It was during the Second World War that we became familiar with the phrase "subversive activity." There is such a thing as "subversive inactivity," which isn't a whole lot better.

Someone has suggested that being a Christian is like riding a bicycle; it's a matter of momentum—if you don't keep going you'll fall off. The story of the Christian and the church is also like riding an escalator. If you aren't going forward, you're going back. What we don't do, what we fail to do, for Christ and his church leaves us and the church slipping behind. Christianity needs our participation to keep from going backwards. St. Paul thought the idea was scandalous, "Some among you are idle; not busy."

Prayer

Make me an active builder of your kingdom. Teach me, holy God, that when I do nothing, I am contributing to the dissolution of your kingdom on earth. Save me from subversive inactivity. Amen.

Try This

Select three areas of Christian work and concern. Pledge that by your activity in them they will survive and be advanced. Be specific about your participation. What, precisely, will you do?

What Good Is It?

What benefit did you reap at that time from the things you are now ashamed of? Those things result in death. Romans 6:21

St. Paul was having his readers hark back to a time when they lived in habitual sin. They would be ashamed to admit to "those things" now that they were Christians. Those were the type of things that resulted in a funeral. When Paul says those things result in death he is thinking spiritual death. But it doesn't take much of a leap in logic to focus on a thing or two of which we would be ashamed to make admission, some of which can and inevitably do end up with our own demise, our physical demise. The point is, Paul's and ours, what does it get you? What's in it for you? Is it worth it?

Looking at it from the humanist's point of view, the things you do which your conscience and most of civilization tells you you shouldn't—sins, in other words—ought to reward you with some kind of pay-off. It costs enough. It costs you your health, your soul, your God, your life. Well, if it costs all that, it ought to pay good dividends, wouldn't you say? Does it? Take an example or two. Drunkenness. What does it profit a man? Hangover, cirrhosis, death. No thanks. Lying. What is the result? Hoist on your own petard. You can have it. Anger. What's the upshot? A black eye, a stressed heart, a lost friendship. Sexual immorality. We've got a whole, new, uncontrolled, devastating disease running wild across our world that's come out of that. Sin is worthless. We ought to know that from our own experience. We all have sinned.

It's not just a matter of not sinning any more. It's a matter of cutting sin out, surgically removing it and its results. That is the specialty of the great surgeon, Christ Jesus, "who gave himself for our sins" (Gal. 1:4). He, not sin, is worth it.

Prayer

Teach me, Son of God, the waste in a life of sin and the gain and glory of a life of righteousness. Help me to choose what benefits my life and my soul, now and in eternity. Amen.

Try This

Scan the first three pages of your morning newspaper and identify those stories with unhappy upshot which are the direct result of self-serving wickedness.

Like a Little Child

Anyone who will not receive the kingdom of God like a little child will never enter it. Mark 10:15

You can believe that. The trouble with being an adult, when it comes to the faith which qualifies one for membership in the kingdom of Christ, is that we grown-ups are all bogged down with, and hedged around by, sophisticated doubts. "How," the blasé want to know, "can these things be?" The virgin birth, the feeding of the five thousand, and the raising of Lazarus are problems for credulity. What doesn't jibe with my own considerable experience is suspect. And the thing that really sticks in the craw, just doesn't want to go down at all, is the idea that our eternal salvation is in his hands, Jesus, the Savior, without any help from us and absolutely no contribution on our part. Children, on the other hand, have no world-wise affectation to frustrate faith or limit expectations.

There is a charming little story coming out of a simpler era which tells about a little boy who went Christmas tree shopping with his grandfather. For hours they went from lot to lot but always the little fellow vetoed his grandfather's selections. Finally, he came out with it. "Grandpa," he said, "I want a tree with lights on it."

Why not? Children expect wonderful things. That's their ticket into the kingdom of God, high hopes and grand expectations—of God. They don't have burdens of doubt to slow them down. They figure, "Nothing is impossible with God" (Luke 1:37). And they figure right.

There is a word of hope to add to this. The older we get the more certain we become that we don't know nearly as much as we thought we did. That already is a grace which clears the way to set it in God's hands, trust him and his power, and stroll into the kingdom of God with our hands in our pockets, we and the children.

Prayer

Make my faith the faith of a child, Lord, my grasp on things eternal the hand of wonderment, and my trust, not in demonstration but in the promises of God. Amen.

Try This

Talk to a four-year-old Christian. Ask her what she believes about Jesus, who he is, what he does. Watch her eyes. Then pray again, "Make my faith the faith of a child."

He Is One of Us

*The Word became flesh and made his dwelling
among us . . . full of grace and truth. John 1:14*

We have surrounded Christ with such an aura, painted him into so many stained glass windows, elevated him over so many altars, that he doesn't seem honest to goodness anymore. He comes off being remote and unreal. When Jesus gets that far away look, remember his word on the cross, "I am thirsty" (John 19:28). That jolts you back to reality. Bone of our bone, flesh of our flesh, and thirsty.

The Old Testament speaks about the hands and feet of God, and scholars smile as if they know something we don't: hands and feet of God. But on the cross you watch God's hands bleed and his feet tear and it's not a laughing matter. God came down from heaven and was made man.

When he came, it wasn't a masquerade party. Mythology presents fascinating stories of the gods taking on human shape and form, often just to check up on us or beat us out of something. But Jesus became man, took on our humanity, and laid aside his glory. He wasn't God slumming for a while among us. He became one of us.

The Word became flesh not just for 33 years, but forever. The incarnation was for keeps. That alters things in a fundamental way. It means we have a warm and understanding friend in the courts of heaven. It means we have an advocate with God who knows all our cares and woes. Brother! That's what he is: your brother. And he sits at God's right hand and runs things. Now there is a comfort for you. Your brother is in charge. Your brother runs the world, your brother who knows just what it's like to be you, not someone remote and unreal, but one who is your brother, and he shall reign forever and ever.

Prayer

My comfort, dear heart, my Savior, is in the knowledge that you have gone through it all and understand. You have gone through it all and were victorious. You have gone through it all for me. I thank and praise you, Lord, and bless your holy name. Amen.

Try This

Think of a disappointment you have endured. Identify a physical pain you live with. Focus on a hope which will no longer materialize in your life. Now think of a comparable disappointment, pain, and shattered hope in Jesus' life.

Living or Dying

If we live, we live to the Lord; if we die, we die to the Lord. Romans 14:8

People are forever paying special attention to the words of those who are dying. They think a person's last words must hold special significance. Jesus' dying words don't measure up to expectations then. They weren't even original. He quoted them from Psalm 31. Everybody knew them. They were sort of the "Now I lay me down to sleep," of his day. "Into your hands I commit my spirit" (Ps. 31:5). "If I should die before I wake, I pray the Lord my soul to take."

Jesus, facing death, approached it the way he faced

life. Going to the hospital and going to bed are not all that different. Jesus accepted the prospect of death as he accepted every event in life. He committed everything to God—big things, little ones, threatening ones, the big one. It just didn't make any difference. All things are in God's hands and we are safe in them.

I like the idea that Jesus' death didn't make any difference to him, since he was in God's hands whether he lived or died. I like even more the idea that Jesus' death makes all the difference in the world to us. Jesus did something when he died, did something for us and to us, did the one thing that counts when you are wheeled in for surgery or lowered gently into the ground. He set us right with God. He washed, cleansed, atoned, freed, forgave; it takes a dictionary to find the words for what was happening, not to Jesus, but to us, on Calvary.

It doesn't matter if it is living or dying you're facing. God's answer and his help is all the same. If you are facing a tense job interview tomorrow, the challenge of a lifetime on Tuesday, severe shooting pains across your chest at the moment, or major surgery at 7:00 a.m. on Friday next, the one, common fact you can rely on is that on the cross "God and sinners reconciled."

Prayer
Dearest Jesus, you were born to be my brother; you lived to be my substitute; you died to be my proxy; you rose to be my king. In life and death, O Lord, you are my hope and stay. Amen.

Try This
Read the following and discover in what situations of life God is "a very present help in trouble." Psalm 40:17; Isaiah 41:10; Isaiah 50:9; Hebrews 13:6.

Forgiven and Forgiving

*But if you do not forgive men their sins, your Father
will not forgive your sins. Matthew 6:15*

It isn't easy to forgive. It doesn't really matter what
the issue is. Whether you are cheated out of $10,000 dol-
lars by a dishonest business partner or slighted at the
church potluck on Tuesday afternoon—it's just not easy to
forgive.

Jesus made it plain that he came to forgive sinners.
He let it be known that he had come to seek and to save
those who are lost. Jesus got right to the heart of matters
with a parable he told about a boy who came home full of
bitter memories and self-recrimination, and was received
with open arms by a forgiving father. Jesus and his life and
death are all about forgiveness.

Nobody needs forgiveness more than we do. We
never seem to believe, really, in the forgiveness of our sins.
We talk about it at church, but then we go home packing
all our guilt along with us, still weighed down.

Maybe we hold on to our guilt because we find it so
hard to forgive others. That's why God gave us the cross,
not just to forgive us for our sins but to show us how it's
done. "Forgive us our trespasses," we pray, "as we forgive
those who trespass against us." Standing under the cross
of Jesus on Calvary, we look up and see that in Christ our
sins have been forgiven. Standing under the cross on Calvary we look up and a strange thing happens to us. Not
only are we forgiven, we walk away forgiving, doing that

which seemed so difficult, remembering the sins and the slights of others no more.

That is the freeing power of forgiveness, to receive it and to exercise it.

Prayer

Dear Lord and great Forgiver, forgive me all my sins, and create that heart in me which in turn forgives my brothers and my sisters, my friends and enemies. In your name I pray. Amen.

Try This

Look squarely into the face of two transgressions which make you feel guilty. Listen to God's grace absolve you of those sins. Identify two things which have been done to you for which someone needs to be forgiven. Forgive as God forgives you.

New in Christ

If anyone is in Christ, he is a new creation.
2 Corinthians 5:17

In a day when Christianity seems rather helpless, really, and people wring their hands over the darkness, gross darkness, which covers the land, we need to take another look at the strong Son of God, and all that he can do for us. He is still the force to make things new. I'd opt to be among his beneficiaries.

On Calvary Jesus hung between two thieves. For all the fact that they were dying, and maybe especially because they were, they were drawn by Jesus' presence to make a decision about him. Up there on Calvary the split was even, one for and one against. It's always like that. Jesus calls on every one to choose. Matthew and Peter and two sisters in Bethany listened to Jesus and followed him. A rich ruler, a whole batch of Pharisees, and most of Jesus' relatives heard Jesus and rejected him. Pontius Pilate thought he would get out of choosing altogether with that silly little ritual with the water and the basin. But Christ demands a response from everyone, and the decision you make matters.

When you confront Christ you have more, however, than just God's challenge to people. You have God's transformation of them. Jesus does more than pique a person's interest. He changes a person's life. One of those thieves on Calvary found himself hanging on a cross, and the next moment, that self-same day we're told, he opened his eyes and he was in paradise. Talk about rags to riches. That is not simply the story of a man being snatched at the last moment from everlasting death for life. That is the story of what Jesus' power can do to a no-good thief. He can make him a saint in the course of the early afternoon. So Saul, the persecutor, becomes Paul, the missionary. Augustine, the early-days playboy, becomes a saint. And, of course, there are you, by the power of the Son of man.

Prayer

I thank you, mighty Redeemer, that you have won me, a lost and condemned creature, and turned me into this child of promise. Let me never despair while with me is faith and your strength and power. Amen.

Try This

Compare some noted nonbelievers with others who have opted for Christ. Which commend themselves? God does a better job of what he makes of people than they can do for themselves.

Free to Serve

Serve the Lord with gladness. Psalm 100:2, KJV

Ah, to be free. One of the things that spoils life is that you have to do this at half past three, or you must be there on Thursday morning. You're the assistant manager at the supermarket. If you didn't have to fit yourself into the boss' way of doing things, your life would be a piece of cake. There are all these constraints and restraints and "have-tos." If only we could be free to go where we wish and do what we want.

Independence! Why is it that once you've got it, you aren't satisfied until you have more? And more. And then some more. We forever want to be free from something. God's purpose is that we be free *for* something. And therein lies a secret. Jesus, on the cross, broke through the chains that bind us. The secret is not in getting away from it all. The secret is in converting all the stifling duties of our existence into grand avenues for accomplishment.

We say Jesus went to the cross voluntarily. Well, the cards were stacked against him. False witnesses put the pressure on. Wicked authorities, knowing him to be innocent, delivered him up to be crucified. Roman soldiers made it inevitable. There were constraints galore. But Jesus took all that tyranny and rose above it. He laid hold of what he was forced to do and used it to fulfill the purpose of his Father for this world. He dedicated his misery and drudgery to the Lord.

I'm suggesting, very practically, that Jesus and the cross show you a way out of the caught and cornered feeling which the responsibilities of life have laid upon you. You simply lay hold of them to use them to do God's will on earth as it is done in heaven. That way you're in charge, free to do what you choose.

Prayer

I would do all things to your glory, Lord, and see every duty as my opportunity to do your will. Amen.

Try This

Dedicate to God each boring task and dreaded responsibility you face today. Do everything you have to do for him. Change "have to" to "want to." Even in this he will set you free.

We Need God

Fear not, for I have redeemed you; I have summoned you by name; you are mine. Isaiah 43:1

God sent his Son into the world "for us men and for our salvation." We don't much like the idea that God thinks we need his Son at all. The confession that our salvation is in him has a way of sticking in our throats. We're perfectly capable of taking care of ourselves. And we are totally serious when we conclude that all our troubles are accidents, and such answers as there are for them will come from us.

The idea that we need no God has flowered in our day, but its roots were laid as far back as the tower they built in the plains of Babel (Genesis 11). They had a hard time getting together in those days and a harder time staying together. So they erected a monument to togetherness, a lofty tower, to demonstrate how, when people join hands and minds and muscle in a common cause, there is nothing which they cannot do. Besides, it was hoped a common goal might minimize some of the fractures which were just then tearing them apart. It takes a lot of pride to work up much of a boast about your basic weakness. But they had enough. So do we.

One of the loudest bangs in the history of this world came when God stuck his pin into that great bag of pride out there in Babel. "The Lord came down to see . . . the tower," the historian confides (Gen. 11:5). If you miss the irony, you miss the point. "This I've got to see," God said, as he bent down and searched around until he finally spied it, that little structure in the valley by which the people thought they had replaced him. And then he scattered them.

We can't get along without God, in time or in eternity. Something outside ourselves is needed "for us men, and for our salvation." And so God sent his Son.

Prayer

Forgive my pride and arrogance, my Lord. You have come to redeem and to renew me precisely because I cannot do that for myself. With gratitude I welcome you and thank and praise your holy name. Amen.

Try This

As you proceed through the day, count the ways—name them specifically, big and little, just for this day, or for your lifetime, or for eternity—in which you are reliant upon God.

The Father of Us All

If you, then . . . know how to give good gifts to your children, how much more will your Father in heaven give good gifts to those who ask him! Matthew 7:11

The world is not an orphanage and all of us its parentless children. Sometimes we feel like it. Here and there someone sings about it: "Sometimes I feel like a motherless child." But there's news to dispel that notion. The world is not a whirling ball hurtling through space, and all of us just accidents upon it. It is home, our home, provided by our father, and we who live here are loved and protected and watched over. From the Bible comes the great news that God loves us as his children. From Calvary and the cross in particular comes news that nothing permanently damaging can happen to us because we are his children. God might create another world, if he wants to, another universe to replace this one, seeing how poorly parts of it have turned out, through no fault of his. But God will not create another you or find anyone else to take your place. You are his own, his child.

Susanna Wesley had 19 children. It's likely she got their clothes mixed. It is not possible she got her children mixed. They never blurred together or blended into each other in her mind. And if one had slipped out of life, she would not have been comforted by the fact that she had 18 more. Her letters show that each had his or her place in her heart.

The heart of God has an eternal place for you. The natives of Africa used to tell David Livingston, when he asked them where the great river goes, "It is lost in the sands." What happens to you, with you, at last? Are you lost in the sands of time? We are not snuffed out forever. We have a father who loves us, who caused his Son to die so that we could live forever, so that we can live with him forever.

Prayer

When I pray "Father" I express my peace in the knowledge that I am a child of the everlasting God. To you, my Father, be glory everlasting. Amen.

Try This

Identify five father-child relationships which, when applied to God and you, give you special comfort.

More than Conquerors

What, then, shall we say in response to this? If God is for us, who can be against us? He who did not spare his own Son, but gave him up for us all—how will he not also, along with him, graciously give us all things? Romans 8:31–32

Wouldn't it be something if you could find one answer which would satisfy every question, one solution which would suffice for every conundrum, one definitive reply which would discharge every cynical doubt?

St. Paul had gotten the word that a little mixed group of Jew and Gentile Christians in Rome was beginning to wonder what good there was in Christianity, why they were going through all sorts of hellish things because of their faith. The whole thing was setting him off his sleep at night. What, he asked himself, are you going to say? What, after all, can you say? It doesn't seem right. Why do the righteous suffer and why do the wicked always seem to get the reward? Finally Paul picked up the pencil, licked the end of it, decided to be a little more formal, (after all, the words had to go down the centuries and stand the test of time), and wrote, "What, then, shall we say in response to this?" And then it came, the perfect answer, the only answer: "If God is for us, who can be against us?" Notice no fancy, philosophical insight, no logical arranging of the facts to suit his purpose. Just the simple fact. God is for us.

Well, that would do it, if it were true. It is. I can prove it. "He did not spare his own Son but gave him up for us all." That does it. Of course, he is for us. The gift of his own Son, his life and death, is all the proof you need. I mean, if he gave up his Son for us all, to die for us, you can count on the rest. "How will he not also, along with him, graciously give us all things?"

Paul could only have come up with that by inspiration, the perfect answer, the satisfying response to every human need or circumstance: "If God is for us, who can be against us."

Prayer

Your love, my Lord, makes me more than conqueror. Amen.

Try This

Ponder the three things that currently trouble you most. In the face of each, apply St. Paul's overarching answer to the question, "What can we say?"

A Quiet Chamber Kept for Thee

The Lord weighs the heart. Proverbs 21:2

Well, that's good news and that's bad news. It's good news because of the alternatives. God could become pre-occupied, for an example, with the things our hands do, or where our feet take us, or what our mouths disgorge on occasion. There are, for a fact, those who earnestly believe that God is interested primarily in what we do, that he's going to make judgments which will affect us eternally on the basis of what his scrutiny of our acts and thoughts and words reveal. So they scurry about to make the investigation come out as positive as possible. But that isn't a very productive exercise. We all have too much knowledge of ourselves, some of the things we have said, some of the things we have done, and a whole lot of places we have gone, to find much comfort in the idea of God rooting around in our history for something to base his eternal judgments upon. When you think of that, there is comfort in the suggestion that God rather weighs the heart.

But that can be bad news too. Look to your heart. Tour around in it. See what God sees. Do you want him putting your innermost prayer life on the scales? How about the secret memories you have stored there, or the vicious feelings you have about this one or that which must forever remain hidden from people around you. The trouble with turning the heart in for God's inspection is that out of the heart come evil thoughts, murder even, immorality, false testimony, slander (Matt. 15:19).

But if God looks to your heart and sees Jesus, if he

weighs it and it measures out as the home of the Savior, then what you have is really good news. Then it's all glad tidings of great joy.

Prayer

Come to my heart, my Savior; make it a quiet chamber kept for thee. Amen.

Try This

Imagine God reviewing three days of last week, your choice. If he weighs those days on the scale of his perfection, where does it leave you? Imagine God turning over and studying two secrets which you have hidden in your heart. If he weighs your heart on the scale of his perfection, where does that leave you? Imagine that God looks to your heart and finds Jesus, that he weighs Jesus upon the scale of his perfection. Where does that leave you?

Here's Hope

He already had in mind what he was going to do.
John 6:6

Out on a hillside in old Palestine, confronted by a throng of hungry people who only had in mind to see a miracle or two, Jesus, for all the fact he solicited suggestions from his closest intimates, had a plan and a solution fast in mind. Recall the story. Jesus, acting baffled, asked, "Where will we buy bread for these people to eat?" He got at least two answers which have armed preachers with ammunition for lectures on faithlessness and sermons on irresponsibility for ages. "Eight months wages wouldn't get the job done." That was one reply. "We've got access to five barley loaves and two limp fish. Woefully inadequate." But Jesus knew what he was going to do.

God knows the answer. Our minds may be befuddled, but there is a mind which isn't. What a heartening thought that is for us in the face of some of the difficult things which threaten us. To know that whatever your problem, whatever the challenge, God knows about it, and while you're still casting about for some solution, some way to gear yourself up for whatever menaces you, God has it figured out. He knows how it will be handled and solved and met, how you are going to come through.

There on that hillside the crowd would be fed. But the disciples had to grope around a little before it would get done. It's the same story for us. The solutions to your problems, whatever they may be, are already determined, and God is simply helping you to find the path out of your woods which he has put there.

Prayer

Guide me, O heavenly King, through the complex problems which beset me. Give me wisdom, strength, and courage for the rigors of my daily life. Above all give me the confidence which comes from knowing that you walk with me and know the path and guarantee that I will make it safely home. Amen.

Try This

Whatever presses you most threateningly at the moment, look to find God's path for you rather than solutions. How can you proceed, living up to his standards and trusting in his promises? Along God's roadways you come upon his answers to your needs.

❖

What's Wrong?

Where does understanding dwell? Job 28:12

What in the world is the matter with me, you ask? Well, that's a big part of it, of course; you're in this world. There's no end to the trouble which comes our way just by reason of the fact that we are alive. And the root of it is this, that there is such a thing as sin and evil and it has spoiled everything, the whole world, and us, too, because we're in it.

You hadn't thought of that? I'm not surprised. It's the nature of this thing called evil that it blinds our eyes and clouds our minds. "It hardens something here within," the poet says. Play the piano eight hours a day, every day, and at the end of the month you ought to know something about playing the piano. But sin for a lifetime, and at the other end of it you won't recognize that it's sin at all. When we are little, we tell a little lie and are almost overpowered by the enormity of it. Then we grow, and our lies grow too. Only our understanding doesn't. It fades, so that when we are full grown, and our lies are full grown, we don't recognize them as lies but call them "business acumen" instead. Nevertheless, it is evil, the evil that people do and that people are, which makes life what it is today. Evil in this world is what is wrong.

Whatever you need to master this world and the evil it brings to your door you can have, if you can squash down your pride and accept it as a gift, a free gift of the religion of Jesus Christ. Is it forgiveness you need? You can have it. All you have to do is lay out your hand palm up. Is it courage you need? The only fight you have is with your own doubts that the "mighty gifts of God" are yours for the taking. For Christ has dealt with evil, redeemed the world, and has taken care of all that is "the matter with" you.

Prayer

Great Redeemer, strong to save, be my savior too. As you redeem the world from evil, spare me from its threat and shame. Amen.

Try This

When a restless mood or depression of spirit overcomes the joy of life and your zest for living, ask God for forgiveness and renewal. Evil is the underlying wrong and only God in Jesus has the answer to it.

He's Here

Surely the Lord is in this place, and I was not aware of it. Genesis 28:16

It came as quite a surprise to Jacob that God was present. It doesn't come as any great surprise to us, however, that Jacob was surprised. He more or less regularly failed to sense the presence of the Lord. One time, in an effort to gain the high ground in what he surmised was going to be a difficult confrontation with his brother Esau, whom he had cheated out of a rightful birthright, Jacob sent every decent defense he had ahead, across the river, in preparation for the morning. Then, that night, alone, all by himself, on his side of the river, there was God, and Jacob had to wrestle with him 'till the breaking of the day.

Jacob did not walk away from that miscalculation. He limped (Gen. 32:22–31).

We too, you and I, fail so often to sense the presence of our Lord. We're too busy making a living, making a fortune, making a life. It's a failing that invites the kind of trouble Jacob got himself into. A lot of our trouble is just God tapping us on the shoulder to remind us he is there, and he is God. That's how you can account for a lot of Jacob's troubles.

And that's how you can account for Jacob's blessings, too, the presence of the Lord: livestock in abundance, black sheep, speckled sheep, and white ones too; reconciliation with his brother; and best of all, the ladder, an open walk-way to the feet of God (Gen. 28:10–22).

God's presence in our lives too: That's how you account for the blessings in them. We rejoice, too, for that prime blessing, an open walkway to the feet of God. "Surely God is in this place," and we ought be aware of it.

Prayer

Accept my prayers of praise, my God, that you are ever with me. When trouble calls me to remember you, help me listen. When blessings come because you are at my side, make me thankful. Amen.

Try This

Name your blessings, one by one. Begin with the best blessing of them all, your adoption as a child of God because of Jesus. See your blessings, each of them, as signals that God is with you.